Letts **explore**

The Catch   Rye

J.D. Salinger

Guide written by Claire Crane and
Juliet Walker

Ruth Welton

A *Letts* **Literature Guide for GCSE**

Contents

Plot summary

1 The narrator, Holden Caulfield, begins his story after suffering from a breakdown. It begins at Pencey Prep school with Holden, having failed his exams, awaiting the Christmas holidays and expulsion.

3 He returns from the evening out and writes an essay for his roommate Stradlater. He is annoyed when Stradlater returns from a date with Holden's old friend, Jane Gallagher. They fight and Holden decides to leave school.

2 Instead of watching a typical Saturday afternoon football game, he visits his old history teacher, Mr Spencer, to say goodbye. In the evening he goes out with two other boys, Mal Brossard and Ackley, an irritating fellow pupil.

9 Holden shouts at Sally and abandons her. He has an unsuccessful meeting with an old friend, Carl Luce and gets very drunk. He wanders through Central Park, alone, thinking of his dead brother, Allie. He accidentally drops Phoebe's record and it smashes. Feeling ill and in despair, he decides to visit his sister.

10 Holden sneaks home and talks to Phoebe. He tells her about his ambition to be the 'Catcher in the Rye'. She gets upset when he says he will run away, so he calls another teacher, Mr Antolini, and visits him.

11 Mr Antolini gives Holden sound advice when he arrives, but after falling asleep Holden is alarmed when he wakes up to find his teacher patting his head. He flees and spends the night in the train station.

5 He visits the Lavender Room – the hotel's night club – and chats and dances with three girls. He is refused alcoholic drinks because he is too young. He then visits Ernie's club in Greenwich Village.

4 Holden gets on a train for New York, and talks to the mother of another Pencey pupil. He arrives at Penn Station in New York, then checks into a seedy hotel and watches guests in other hotel rooms from his window.

6 After leaving the club he goes back to the hotel and arranges a meeting with a prostitute, Sunny. He has second thoughts and she leaves after being paid. Sunny's pimp arrives and beats up Holden for not giving them more money.

8 Holden and Sally meet but he hates the theatre show. They go ice-skating and Holden gets very depressed and intense. He asks Sally to run away with him and get married. Sally refuses Holden's offer.

7 Feeling lonely, he calls an ex-girlfriend called Sally Hayes. They arrange to meet the next afternoon to go to the theatre. The next morning Holden talks to two nuns while having breakfast at Grand Central Station. He gives them a large donation. He then buys his sister, Phoebe, a record.

12 Holden meets Phoebe the next day for lunch and she asks if she can run away with him. He refuses. She is upset so he takes her to the zoo and she plays on the carousel. Seeing Phoebe so happy, Holden decides not to run away but to return home. The story ends with him saying he misses everyone.

Who's who in *The Catcher in the Rye*

Holden Caulfield

Holden is the narrator of the story, its protagonist. He is the youngest son (since his brother died) of a wealthy New York family. He has an older brother, D.B. and a younger sister, Phoebe. An intense, thoughtful boy, he has become increasingly disaffected since the death of his younger brother, Allie, from leukemia, when Holden was 13. Since then he has moved from boarding school to boarding school, either as a result of being expelled for failing classes or because he has become fed up with the number of 'phonys' and has chosen to leave.

Holden seems to be a typical, hormonal, teenage boy – unsure about girls, tired of society's falseness and hypocrisy, and a loner. He is fiercely cynical about the environment around him, whether it be the expensive private schools he is sent to, successful businessmen, movie stars or even his successful writer brother D.B., who has moved to Hollywood.

An unusual-looking boy, Holden claims he is handsome, but not in a traditionally glamorous way, like his roommate Stradlater. He is tall for his age (16) and one side of his hair is prematurely grey. He bemoans his lack of success with girls, but emotionally does not seem ready for any kind of physical relationship. He says he finds girls confusing because you never know what they are thinking, but in truth, he probably scares them away with his intensity. After meeting Sally, for example, he asks her to marry him, even after a fairly unsuccessful date.

Holden is a complex character and one who has been deeply scarred by the death of his brother, who he talks about in wholly positive terms. In fact, he talks about most young children this way, illustrating that perhaps it is the act of growing up that he is finding traumatic. His personality is a mass of contradictions. The hypocrisy he loathes in others, for example, is readily shown when he lies throughout the weekend. Similarly, he hates people who are affected, but he puts on many guises himself (claiming to have a tumour to gain sympathy, pretending to be shot, saying he is 22 and so on).

By the end of the novel, the character traits that Holden reveals at the start of the weekend have developed into a dangerous set of negative and emotional responses. He is close to suicide and he has become physically weak; he cannot sleep, has stomach aches, faints and cannot stop himself bursting into tears on several occasions, through despair. It is clear that he is a very sensitive boy who is still greatly troubled by events in his past. He admits that when he first heard the news about Allie he smashed all the windows in his parents' garage, and says that there were suggestions that he be psychoanalysed. This clearly never happened, and we now see a teenager who has struggled for at least three years with these thoughts, and who has never really come to terms with his loss. He still talks aloud to Allie as if he is there and he admits to Phoebe that even though he is dead Allie is still one of the people he likes best.

The fact that his emotional development has been stunted in this way could account for his bad smoking habit, and his inability to make close friends or to feel part of a team. He would rather be an outsider. This is reflected in his bizarre ambition to be a 'catcher in the rye'. This dream is symbolic – the only thing Holden believes he can find satisfaction doing is waiting for small children to fall into danger so he can rescue them. This surely reflects his longing to have been able to save his brother. It also reveals how he believes children should be protected.

Despite his troubles, Holden is not an easy character to sympathise with. He is negative, he moans all the time and he is very frustrating. He will not face up to his future or his responsibilities and he refuses to take advice. By the end of the novel we are still not convinced that he has made any progress in this area. We can only hope that any genuine suicidal tendencies have been stemmed.

Phoebe

Phoebe is ten years old and is Holden's younger sister. She is the family member to whom he is most close now that Allie has died, and it is largely for her sake that he returns home. She is very fond of him and is concerned about him. Holden considers that she has sense and understanding beyond her years. She looks attractively skinny and pretty, with reddish hair. She is intelligent, emotional and affectionate, and enjoys writing stories. She is someone Holden always feels like talking to on the phone, but he does not call her, because it is unlikely that she will be the one to answer. In some ways she is a typical child, enjoying roller skating and taking pride in learning to belch, but in other ways she is sophisticated – keeping her possessions very neat and tidy and trying to watch over Holden. When he tells her that he has broken the record he had bought for her, she stores the pieces away like treasure, as if throwing them away would be discarding a part of Holden.

Phoebe is perceptive, and she talks to Holden as if she were the older one, telling him not to swear and talking about his failure at school. She is the one who makes him face up to the fact that he is dissatisfied with everything and must not always rely on people, like Allie, who are no longer alive. She also puts him right about the words of the 'Coming through the Rye' poem, destroying his more innocent impression of it. She also generously lends Holden her Christmas spending money.

It is interesting that Holden gives his precious hunting hat to her, and strangely appropriate, since Phoebe was one of the names of the goddess of hunting in Greek and Roman mythology. She petulantly throws it back to him after a disagreement, but then tenderly, even maternally, puts it on his head, to protect him from the rain. It is she who is responsible for putting an end to his restless quest – he sits happily watching her on the carousel, a ride that significantly she feels she has grown out of, until he is ready to go home to begin resolving his problems.

Allie

Allie, who died from leukaemia when he was 11, is Holden's younger brother by two years. Holden was badly affected by his death three years ago. Allie was distinctive in appearance, having bright red hair, and also stood out by being left handed, which was less common at that time, and for writing in green ink. He is described as a thoroughly nice and well-adjusted boy. He also seems to have been very intelligent, working hard at school. Even tempered, despite his fiery hair, Allie also had a good sense of humour. He was unusual for a child, because he had written poems on his baseball mitt so that he had something to read during lulls in the game. Allie still occupies Holden's thoughts and it helps him to talk aloud to Allie when he is depressed. In a way, Allie is Holden's saviour in his weakest moments. Part of Allie's enduring appeal for Holden is that he is frozen in time, like the exhibits in the Museum, and he is forever in the innocence of childhood.

D.B.

D.B. (we do not find out his full name) is Holden's older brother. He is in his twenties and lives in Hollywood, where he is a writer of film scripts. He earns a great deal of money, drives a Jaguar and has a good-looking English actress girlfriend. He does not appear in the novel, but is mentioned by Holden on the first and last page, which indicates his importance to him, even if he does criticise D.B.'s lifestyle.

Sally Hayes

Sally Hayes is an ex-girlfriend of Holden's from New York, with whom he is still in contact. He keeps a picture of her in his room at Pencey Prep, probably because she is very good looking. She goes to college and comes from a well-off background. Her parents are not impressed with Holden because of his wildness. Holden does not consider Sally to be very intelligent, nor to be able to hold a decent conversation. She is very interested in image. She thinks it is time that Holden grew his hair, because crew cuts are not the style of the moment. She is a conscious dresser, looking dramatic in a black coat and beret when she arrives for the date with him. Later she wants to skate, even though she has no skill at it, because it gives her the opportunity to pose in a short skating skirt.

Sally is aware of her power to attract men and talks at length to Holden on the phone about others who are interested in her, perhaps trying to make him jealous. In the theatre interval she appears shallow, trying to make an impression and scanning the crowd, rather than talking to Holden. She seems fond of him, but does not understand him. She makes the mistake of telling him that perhaps he does not understand what he is talking about either, which provokes him into insulting her. This makes her furious and upset, because up to now she has only been treated with respect by boys. She is high on Holden's list of 'phonies', but she is sensible enough to see the absurdity of his suggestions of elopement and marriage.

Ward Stradlater

Stradlater is Holden's roommate at Pencey. Immediately we see that he embodies the type of boy the school is proud to nurture. Although Holden claims he is conceited and arrogant, he defends him saying that he is generous and friendly. Holden never describes Stradlater as 'phony', but this character has strong elements of artificiality about him. On the surface he is a very good-looking boy, but he only has a photographic charm. He borrows a jacket from Holden, even though he might stretch it with his big shoulders, and wanders around half naked to show off his good figure.

Outwardly Stradlater is friendly and considerate to Holden, but he is self-obsessed and arrogant. Stradlater is a slob in secret, who insists on shaving before a date so he looks immaculate, but uses a razor that is in a disgusting, filthy state. This character seems to be just as 'phony' as all the others at Pencey. Holden admires his generosity and his looks, which are just two ways that Stradlater creates a 'public persona'. It is significant that Ackley, who Holden dismisses early on as being false and irritating, sees through Stradlater and cannot bear to be in the same room as him.

Unlike Holden, Stradlater is clearly very successful with girls, but his lack of real concern for his girlfriends is shown by the fact that he cannot even remember his date's name and calls her Jean instead of Jane. Because of Stradlater's reputation as a stud, Holden becomes very concerned about the welfare of Jane when he returns later, but in a redeeming way he refuses to talk about it. Ironically, and probably by design, the fact that he does not tell Holden any details, means that Holden assumes the worst and Stradlater's reputation is held up.

We see Stradlater through the perspective of Holden, and we understand that he is a 'jock' – good looking, sporty and a hit with the girls – a typical 'All-American Boy'. He is used to getting his own way, either through charm or persistence, and has no qualms about getting Holden to write his homework for him. His character is not wholly negative, though. He is generous and friendly to Holden, but one suspects this is mostly due to what he can get from him. In this chapter alone Stradlater borrows Holden's jacket, hair gel, old girlfriend and his writing talent.

Mr Antolini

Mr Antolini was Holden's English teacher at one of his previous schools, Elkton Hills, and now lives and works in New York. He appears to be happily married to an older, well-off woman, and lives in a smart neighbourhood near the East River. He appears towards the end of the novel, in Chapter 24, and offers a contrast to the history teacher, Mr Spencer. Both teachers can see that Holden is heading for trouble, but Mr Antolini's advice is not scorned, because Holden respects him and feels that he can relate to him. This is not just because he is fairly young – probably in his late twenties to early thirties – but because he does not behave like a typical figure of authority. He drinks heavily, makes jokes (and not at Holden's expense), and Holden feels that he can ring him in the middle of the night. Holden does not see him as a phony, but as a caring individual; after all, it was he who took the initiative to tend to the body of the suicide victim, James Castle.

Mr Antolini feels that Holden is riding for a fall – recalling the image of catching. He recognises how troubled he is and tries to explain that he is not the only one who has felt like this and that a good education will help him become who he wants to be. He is obviously genuinely concerned about Holden, who he considers to be a very strange boy. This makes it very unlikely, unless you take a cynical view, that he would make homosexual advances, as Holden suspects when he wakes in the night to find Mr Antolini patting him on the head. This is more like the gesture of an affectionate and protective father to a child.

Jane Gallagher

Jane represents Holden's ideal girl. Although we never see her directly in the story, we are first introduced to her as Stradlater's date for the evening. She used to be Holden's next door neighbour in Maine, and they became close friends two summers ago. Holden constantly reminisces about spending time with her and she is one of the few people that he speaks about in positive terms. Holden describes her as attractive, but not classically beautiful. He says he likes the way she talks quickly and the way her mouth moves when she gets excited about something.

Their relationship was entirely platonic, which may be one of the reasons Holden is so sentimental about her. Apart from a little hand-holding and a gentle closeness between them, there was nothing physical to ruin their relationship. In fact, they way he describes the time they spent together – playing golf, tennis and checkers – it sounds like a very innocent, childhood friendship. Holden is happy with this idealised image, and it is one of the reasons he becomes so angry with Stradlater, whom he knows is a sexual predator – Holden cannot bear to think of Jane in such terms.

Jane symbolises a <u>beacon</u> <u>of</u> <u>light</u> <u>and</u> <u>hope</u> for Holden throughout the novel. He is constantly trying to reach her or talk to her, but he can never bring himself to do so. When she arrives at Pencey he says he is not in the mood to talk to her, and although he thinks about calling her several times, he never manages to find the courage to do so. Because of this, <u>Jane</u> <u>remains</u> <u>a</u> <u>perfect</u> <u>image</u> <u>of</u> <u>his</u> <u>past</u> and, although he strives to bring her into his future, he ultimately fails in this endeavour.

Robert Ackley

Ackley is a fellow pupil at Pencey Prep who has the room next door to Holden. He is described as <u>irritating</u> <u>and</u> <u>obnoxious</u> and he has revolting personal habits. He cuts his nails in Holden's room, rarely brushes his teeth and he also has terrible skin. In some ways, however, he is like Holden. His views annoy people, he is a blatant liar and <u>he</u> <u>is</u> <u>a</u> <u>fellow</u> <u>loner</u> <u>who</u> <u>craves</u> <u>company</u>.

Ackley is a figure of fun at Pencey, and at one stage Holden says he found it cruel that the other students were so horrible to him. In one of his better moments, Holden feels so sorry for Ackley that he invites him out on Saturday with his other friend to go to the movies.

Like Stradlater, <u>Ackley</u> <u>represents</u> <u>a</u> <u>typical</u> <u>type</u> <u>of</u> <u>student</u>. He is not good looking, does not have many friends, pretends he is sexually experienced when he clearly isn't, and is generally an irritating character. Ackley and Stradlater are polar opposites. Holden fits somewhere between the two. The fact that he is more like Ackley may be one of the reasons why Holden has so little patience with him.

Mr Spencer

Mr Spencer is Holden's history teacher from Pencey Prep. He represents a kind of father figure; older, wise and full of good advice. Holden, however, on this occasion, is a little revolted that Mr Spencer is recovering from 'flu and the house smells of ill people. Mr Spencer puts Holden on the spot and questions him about his plans and whether he has any ambition. He reads aloud Holden's poor history examination paper and makes him feel ashamed of his academic failings and lack of dedication. He advises him to get more direction and focus in his life. Mr and Mrs Spencer are clearly worried about Holden and only want the best for him. Mr Spencer, in particular, seems to despair of Holden's lack of academic motivation, but the meeting ends positively with him wishing Holden good luck for the future.

Mr and Mrs Caulfield

Holden's parents live comfortably on the 12th floor of an apartment block on 71st Street, near Central Park. His father is a lawyer, and there is obviously no shortage of money, for they have a maid, Phoebe has smart clothes and Holden has expensive leather luggage bought for him. Neither parent directly appears in the novel. We see no evidence of them supporting Holden, though they had considered psychiatric help for him after Allie's death and his father has recently voiced his concerns about him to Mr Antolini. Holden tells us that his father thinks he is immature. The loss of their youngest son, Allie, has hit them hard. They visit his grave frequently with flowers, and his mother is still in a nervy state; Holden says that she reacts hysterically to bad news, gets frequent headaches and does not much enjoy social events. He worries how they will respond to news of yet another failure at school.

Famous for not wanting to be famous *

J. D. Salinger

Jerome David ('Jerry') Salinger was born on New Year's Day 1919 in New York, where he lived for his childhood years. His father became successful in the cheese importing business, so the family were able to move from the West Side to the smarter East Side, the Caulfield's neighbourhood. Several aspects of Salinger's early life are reflected in *The Catcher in the Rye*. In his early teenage years Salinger, like Holden, was manager of his school fencing team. He excelled in dramatic productions, but was lazy in academic work. From the age of 15 he was sent to a military academy, probably the basis for Pencey Prep, which is where he started writing.

Salinger went fleetingly to university, but decided to be a writer or, failing that, an actor. He was a tall, dark and striking-looking young man, who even did a season as an entertainer on a Caribbean cruise ship. His father hoped he would enter the import business, so sent him to Europe to improve his foreign languages and to learn the ham trade. Salinger was not enthusiastic about this and all the time sent stories back to magazines in the States. His father eventually had to admit defeat, and Salinger had his first story published when he was 20.

In the Second World War Salinger was drafted into the army and posted to Devon in England, from where he became involved in the D-Day landings in France. He suffered some sort of breakdown at the end of the war and remained in France for a time. His first marriage, which lasted eight months, was to a French girl. His second marriage, which ended in divorce in 1967, produced two children. One of his

*Quotation from Ian Hamilton, *In Search of JD Salinger* (1988)

early girlfriends left him to marry the much older Charlie Chaplin.

Salinger worked on a novel featuring Holden Caulfield on and off for many years, but only published short stories in the 1940s. He had various quarrels with editors because he wanted control over his work, and did not want a single word of text to be edited or deleted. He objected to illustrated covers and insisted on writing his own biographical details.

Despite having an encyclopaedic knowledge of the movies, and reportedly a vast collection of 1940s films, Salinger in some ways despised the film industry – as you can see from Holden's comments in his novel. In 1950 he allowed a screenplay to be developed from one of his stories, under the new title *My Foolish Heart*, and was very cross with himself later for allowing it to happen, because it was a tear jerking melodrama which made a mockery of his work. He has made sure that *The Catcher in the Rye* has never been filmed, although many directors would have welcomed the chance to tackle it.

The Catcher in the Rye was eventually published to great acclaim in July 1951. Salinger did not want his picture on the cover and did not like the fuss that followed publication, so retreated to a cottage in Cornish, New Hampshire. Everything Salinger wrote from the mid-1950s focused on a fictional family called Glass, including *Franny and Zooey*, two short stories published in book form, which was a bestseller for six months. The last time any new work appeared in print was a long short story published in the New Yorker magazine in 1965. Little is known about Salinger from this date, because he lives reclusively and does not welcome intrusions on his privacy. He refuses all interviews, photographs and opportunities to be published. He has shown contempt for publishers, literary critics and biographers because he feels that they have, in the past, taken advantage of him. *He will not allow quotations from his books to be used in other printed material.* He is apparently still writing, but it is possible, regrettably, that no one will ever read what he has produced.

What sort of novel is *The Catcher in the Rye*?

The technical name for this type of novel is a *bildungsroman* – a German term, literally meaning a 'development novel'. Books in this genre deal with a person's – usually a young man's – formative years and development to maturity. Examples include *David Copperfield* and *Huckleberry Finn*. *The Catcher in the Rye* is only partly this sort of book, because Holden does not reach maturity by the end of it, and the action covers only three days. It does, however, deal with some of the problems of adolescence.

The development of the novel

Salinger had been writing about a character called Holden Caulfield for about ten years before *The Catcher in the Rye* was published in 1951. He admitted that Holden was a self-portrait and apparently used to talk about him, and quote from him, as if he were a real person. Holden featured in two short stories in the mid-1940s, *Slight Rebellion off Madison* and *I'm Crazy*, which deal with episodes found in the novel. In these early versions Holden was not so fully developed or distinctive.

Teenagers

It has been said that Holden Caulfield is the first modern teenager in fiction, though that term was not in common use at the time of publication. Certainly before the Second World War adolescents were not considered as a group of people in their own right and their problems were not discussed. These issues were brought to the fore in the 1950s with films like James Dean's *Rebel Without a Cause* and with the rise of rock and roll. The novel had enormous impact at a time when young people were beginning to question the accepted way of doing things and to rebel against conventional middle-class lives and attitudes. It provided a focus for them, with Holden becoming something of a role model, and became essential reading for college students.

Reactions to the novel

The novel was an instant success when it was published in 1951 and most reviews were favourable, praising it for its newness of tone and style. The *New York Times* called it: 'an unusually brilliant first novel'. It reached cult status among students in the 1960s and has always sold well, with over 250,000 copies still being bought annually. It has also frequently been controversial, mainly because of Holden's language. It was not until the 1990s that it was published in the UK with all the taboo words retained. Further notoriety was caused in 1980, when Mark Chapman, the assassin of ex-Beatle John Lennon, asked Lennon to sign a copy of the novel on the morning of the killing.

New York

In the 19th century New York was organised into its present rectangular grid system, with the exception of Broadway, which followed an old Native American trail down the length of Manhattan Island. The streets and avenues were numbered, with the Caulfield home, on 71st Street, situated on the east side of Central Park, near Fifth Avenue. The city was bustling, even in the 1940s, as you can tell from Holden's visit to Broadway, where the crowds make him feel claustrophobic. There was a large elevated rail system, which has since been replaced by the subway, and two main stations, Grand Central and Penn. The old Penn station building, Holden's arrival point in the city, was pulled down in the early 1960s. There was not such a density of buildings and fewer skyscrapers in the 1940s. After the Second World War there was much development on landfill sites, including the area where the Twin Towers of the World Trade Centre were built. In the novel we are given no sense of the political or economic situation in the United States, but Holden socialises with affluent people.

Penn Station, Holden's arrival point in New York.

Falseness

Holden expounds on the notion of falseness, hypocrisy or, as he calls it, 'phoniness' throughout the text. It is an idea he introduces in the very first chapter, and he accuses D.B.'s new girlfriend of it in the very last paragraph. His loathing of hypocrisy is more than a teenage idiosyncrasy. He has honed his skills of observation to such a degree that he can spot elements of it in virtually anyone he meets. Naturally, the privileged schools he has been sent to are crammed with 'phonies', from roommates to ex-pupils, and anyone who is part of the entertainment business displays some falseness, primarily from the requirement to put on an act. He cites singers, friends, girlfriends and random strangers as all being affected by this nasty quality.

The huge irony, of course, is that Holden is just as guilty of being false as anyone else. He does not hesitate to lie to Mrs Morrow when he meets her on the train, telling her he has a tumour. He lies constantly about his age so that he can buy alcohol, and he lies to Mr Spencer and Mr Antolini when he needs an escape route. The fact that he is such a consummate liar could be one of the reasons why he finds falseness so easy to detect in others, but also why he hates it so much. It may also be one of the reasons why he feels so comfortable with younger children. In his eyes, they are less guilty of falseness and are more true to themselves. Essentially, this is what Holden strives for. He does not have the maturity to understand that we need a certain amount of protection, which comes from telling white lies or from playing a role from time to time. If you strip yourself bare and are completely honest, you are very vulnerable. The reason he is so happy to talk to the two nuns is because he sees them, like children, as being free from affectation and, therefore, completely open and honest.

Growing up

Holden's confused state has a great deal to do with his attitude towards growing up. He is 16 and therefore on the edge of adulthood. His height and greying hair suggest that he is already grown up, but his lack of emotional maturity contradict this. Most of the people he meets bring up the subject of his age, either questioning whether he is old enough to be drinking alcohol or thinking it is time that he grew up. On one hand he despises the adult world, which he thinks is full of phonies, but on the other he tries to imitate it by taking part in its activities. He certainly does not understand it and is fearful of the loss of childhood innocence.

Holden is wary of change, as you can tell from his attitude to the Museum of Natural History. He remembers happy childhood visits there and sees it as a cosy refuge from the outside world. He likes the fact that you can rely on the exhibits, like the Indians and the Eskimo, to always be the same. He is saddened by the thought of regular visitors changing slightly with each visit, including Phoebe, who is gradually growing up. As he thinks about these changes he puts on his hunting hat, as if to protect himself. He decides not to visit the museum, perhaps because it would mean that he would have to come to terms with the changes in himself.

In his wish to become the catcher in the rye, Holden sees himself as the protector of childhood innocence. He has a good opinion of children and never criticises them for being phony, even if they sometimes mimic adults in their behaviour. The field of rye is seen as the landscape of childhood with the cliff (which implies danger, even death) being the route to adulthood. At the end of the novel, when Phoebe is on the carousel, Holden suddenly understands that you cannot always protect children. You have to let them experience some danger and to find their own limits. You cannot always stop them from falling. This realisation means that Holden is now almost ready to move on. Ironically, his first action in this enlightened state is to return home, where he can be looked after by his parents.

Communication

Holden has a desperate need to communicate with other people, particularly since he is often lonely and depressed, but he lacks the ability to do so. In most cases he either backs away from contacting people or ruins everything when he does, because nothing is straightforward to him. Even one of his more successful encounters, with the nuns at Grand Central Station, concludes with him unintentionally blowing cigarette smoke into their faces.

It is not only telephone communication that Holden shuns, but face-to-face contact as well. He repeatedly says he ought to go down and say hello to Jane Gallagher, when she is at Pencey Prep waiting to go on a date with Stradlater, but he does not do so. Perhaps subconsciously he wants to remember and preserve the good relationship he had with her 18 months before and knows that things are bound to change if he sees her again. Twice, in bars, he even sends messages to the performers asking them to join him for a drink, which shows his urgent need to connect with someone.

Holden is rarely stuck for words – indeed, English is the only subject that he does not fail – but he tells Mr Antolini that he realises he is very hard to talk to. When he is depressed the person he talks aloud to is his dead brother, Allie; a one-way conversation, which is all he seems to be able to manage. Near the end of the book he even considers pretending to be a deaf-mute if he runs away, so that he does not have to have stupid and meaningless conversations with anyone. His obsession with communication is shown by it being the subject of the last paragraph of the novel, when he advises the reader not to tell anyone about anything they have been through, or they will start missing everyone they mentioned. Holden's problem is that the one thing he craves is always destroyed by his troubled mental state.

Relationships

Relationships, closely linked to the theme of communication, are difficult for Holden to establish. His journey from Pencey Prep to his home in New York, gives an insight to his relationships with school friends, strangers from different walks of life, old friends and mentors, and family. We see his fascination with – and yet unreadiness for – sexual relationships and his reliance on contacts from the past. He is frightened of moving forward and yet cannot cope with the present.

The first phase of the book deals with Holden's relationship with fellow pupils. He has friends at Pencey, but his interaction with them is not straightforward. He expresses to Ackley, another boy at the school, the desire to join a monastery. this may be because there he would be forced to live a life with only spiritual relationships.

When Holden arrives in New York, on the second stage of his journey, he stays on the West Side, to make sure that he is away from his home territory and therefore in little danger of running into anyone he knows. He feels unready to re-establish long-standing relationships, hence his inability to contact old friends by phone. His intention to stay there for a few days, until his parents have accepted the fact that he has failed at yet another school, is foiled by his failure to relate to the people that he meets, leading him to cut the visit short.

In the next section of the novel, Holden meets old friends of both sexes, with little success. The friends annoy Holden, and Holden annoys them; this is true of both Sally Hayes and Carl Luce. Holden feels he is always being let down by people who should be able to help him and now expects disappointment. He finishes the evening sitting alone in Central Park – he cannot even find any ducks there – and thinks he is going down with pneumonia. This, at least, directly leads to the final stage, re-establishing his relationship with Phoebe.

Phoebe puts an end to his restless quest. Towards the end of the novel, sitting still and watching Phoebe going round on the carousel, he is happy and ready to return home. In the last chapter though, when he is receiving medical help, we see that he is still uneasy in his dealings with people, because he feels that they ask too many questions. This, ironically, is one of Holden's own faults, leading to the breakdown of his relationships with various characters through the novel.

Individuality

One of the qualities Holden most seems to like about himself and others is their willingness to be seen as individuals. Holden is happy to be individual, despite the fact that it is unusual in a teenager and may be laughable on occasion. Unfortunately, because of this desire to stand alone and not be one of the crowd, Holden's individuality often makes him feel isolated and lost. Ultimately, to be content as an individual you need to have a strong character, and Holden is not really mentally robust enough.

Holden's delight in his bright red hunting hat is one of the outward manifestations of his desire to be unique, and it is admired by many different people throughout the novel. The fact that he takes his hat on and off according to his circumstances means that his individuality fluctuates with his bravery. However, his desire to be independent means that he is often lonely. At the start of the novel we see him, alone, on the brow of a hill, overlooking a football game. We could never imagine Holden actually taking part in such a team sport. The same drive to be an individual is why he could not bear to be in the Scouts. He claims that he could not stand staring at the neck of the boy in front when they stood in line.

A sense of being an individual and standing up for your own beliefs is why Holden has such admiration for the martyr, James Castle. It is also why he respects Mr Antonlini – the only person with enough courage and integrity to pick up James' body after his death. As the novel progresses, Holden's sense of individuality lessens and he increasingly requires support from his family, old colleagues, an imaginary Allie and even the 'kindness of strangers' – the nuns and the kind hat-check girl.

The hunting hat

Holden buys a red hunting hat, with an extremely long peak and flaps to cover the ears, in a shop in New York immediately after leaving the fencing equipment on the train. He has let down his team, who are annoyed with him, and wearing this hat is both a statement of his individuality and a form of protection from the outside world. The hat gives as confusing a picture as Holden himself. It is scarlet in colour, therefore very obvious and distinctive, yet a hat worn for hunting purposes would be more effective if it provided camouflage. Although Holden sometimes wants to be isolated, conversely he draws attention to himself through his outrageous behaviour. He is proud of the hat and conscious of what he is doing with it, particularly in the first part of the novel. At this time, the only person who would wear a hat with the peak to the back was the catcher, the key player in the team, to enable him to fit his mask on his face without obstruction. This is interesting, because it links the hunting hat to the idea of the catcher in the rye, another motif.

Holden tells Ackley that it is not a deer-shooting hat, but a people-shooting one. However, he is not always so defiant. When he is nervous he turns the peak to the front, as if to hide his face. He puts the hat on at key moments, such as when he leaves Pencey, (this time with the peak resolutely to the back).

When Holden gives the hat to Phoebe, it is a sign that he is relying on it less as a defence against the outside world. When she comes to meet him at the museum the next day, he is able to recognise her from a distance, because of the colour; this links with the time that he spotted Allie from far off on his bike, just because of his bright red hair. There is another link: Allie's presence is made more real to Holden because he owns his glove. Maybe this is why he also gives Phoebe an item of clothing, so that if he dies she can wear it and, in some way, still be close to him. At the end, when they are at the carousel, she affectionately puts the hat on Holden's head because it has started to rain. He comments that the hat gave him quite a lot of protection from the rain, but through the book we can see that it has provided shelter from much more than the weather.

The baseball glove

Allie's baseball glove is one of Holden's most treasured possessions. He takes it with him to boarding school, much in same way that others might take photographs of their family or a teddy bear. It brings him comfort and gives him a tangible connection to his dead brother. He describes the fielder's mitt as being covered in poems. It is an extremely personal item – the fact that Jane Gallagher is one of the few people he has shared it with indicates the closeness of their relationship.

There is a connection between this item and Holden's greatest ambition – to be the catcher in the rye. He explains to Phoebe how he would like to stand on the edge of a cliff, waiting to catch young children if they were in danger of falling. Allie's death seems to have sparked in Holden a desire to protect other children from any kind of emotional pain, which is symbolised by their falling off a metaphorical cliff.

Holden writes about the baseball glove at the start of the story, when Stradlater asks him to write an essay that has to be descriptive. He cannot see that this is an inappropriate choice for an essay topic, but we should note that up until now, very few people have seen this glove. The fact that he wishes to write about it in a public forum could be seen to be his very first cry for help in the novel. Unfortunately, it is dismissed by Stradlater and Holden ends up throwing the shredded essay in the bin. As readers, too, we do not necessarily see the importance of this choice early in the novel.

Ducks

The question of where the ducks go in winter, when the lagoon in Central Park freezes, may have occurred to Holden in his childhood when, he tells us, he knew the park like the back of his hand. However, it begins to bother him this weekend, since he is feeling restless and unstable. He starts thinking about the ducks while Mr Spencer is questioning him about his failure in school subjects. He goes on to ask two separate taxi drivers if they can explain the ducks' whereabouts. Because it seems like the question of a child, but is coming from a young man travelling to adult locations, they suspect he is having fun at their expense.

The absence of the ducks bothers Holden, because he does not like change or sudden disappearance. Allie was suddenly no longer there, but the ducks come back in the spring, showing an affirmation of new life. Thinking about the man who may come to rescue the ducks possibly contributes to Holden's idea about becoming the catcher in the rye, the rescuer of children.

In a drunken state, Holden tries to find the lagoon at night, to check on the ducks. When he eventually locates the pond, there are no ducks and it is partly frozen. It is in a kind of limbo, between flowing water and ice, as is Holden, who is poised between the worlds of childhood and adulthood. Holden almost falls into the water while searching for the ducks, which links with Mr Antolini's idea that he is in danger of heading for a great fall in life.

The 'Little Shirley Beans' record

This record, like Holden's quest for answers concerning the ducks in Central Park, is another of his obsessions. One of the recurring images in the book is the notion of going full circle. Phoebe spends time on the carousel, a record spins round and Holden's story ends as it begins, with him in recovery. He initially hears the record at Pencey and likes it so much he tries to buy it from one of the boys. The boy refuses to sell it so Holden is determined to find it for Phoebe, even though it is an old record and quite rare. (The singer, Estelle Fletcher, is a real singer from the time, but the song is Salinger's invention.) The record links with the theme of childhood and growing up, because it is a ballad about a young girl who is too ashamed to go out because she has just lost her two front teeth.

In one of the very few positive events in the story Holden actually manages to find the record in the very first shop he goes to. At this point we believe that perhaps things will start to improve for him, especially as he now has a reason to see his younger sister and, perhaps, go home. It is doubly tragic, therefore, that in his darkest hour, having got drunk and been abandoned by his friend, he stumbles in a deserted Central Park and smashes the record. It symbolises his loss of any hope for the future, and the fact that his own childhood is finally at an end. This is his rite of passage. The importance of the record to Holden is demonstrated when he carefully picks up the pieces and puts them in his pocket, even though he knows they are useless.

A hint of salvation comes later when Holden finally visits Phoebe. As if realising their value, she takes the shattered pieces of vinyl from Holden and stows them safely in her bedside cabinet drawer, saying that she likes to save them. Like Holden, she understands, without being told, how important they are. To her, the pieces of record are a symbol of Holden's love for her and so she treasures them.

The Catcher in the Rye

Robert Burns' 19th-century song, *Comin' Thro' The Rye*, is the inspiration for the title of the novel and for Holden's wish to become the catcher in the rye when he is older. Burns adapted an old song, cleaning up the lyrics, but even so the song is about two people who meet in a field for a sexual encounter. Holden has misheard, or misremembered the lyrics, and thinks it is 'If a body *catch* a body', when he hears the little boy in New York singing it. He might be deliberately blanking out the sexual implications, which would tally with his resistance to growing up, and ironically it takes a child, his sister Phoebe, whose innocence he wants to protect, to point out his mistake.

When Holden hears the little boy in New York singing, it makes him feel less depressed because the boy is singing for the sake of singing, not because he has to or is out to impress someone. Holden recalls the song when Phoebe asks him what he would like to be. He chooses a career of his own making, that of the catcher in the rye: a person who catches children before they fall over a cliff at the edge of the field of rye where they are playing.

The idea of falling recurs through the novel, from the physical falls of Holden down steps as he leaves Pencey and later almost into the lake in Central Park, to Mr Antolini's worry that Holden is heading for a terrible metaphorical fall. Holden also hallucinates that he will fall ever downwards as he crosses the road and will never reach the other side. It is Allie, perhaps wearing his baseball mitt, who he calls on for help. Catching links with the motifs of the hunting hat worn backwards, like the catcher's cap in baseball, and with Allie's baseball mitt.

Text commentary

Chapters 1 to 7

Chapter I

Chapter 1 starts with the main character, Holden Caulfield, establishing a close relationship with the reader. He begins in a casual, blasé way, suggesting that we are friends, perhaps, and have been urging him to tell us his story. His tone is dismissive and slightly sarcastic, and he declares that he has no wish to follow the traditional, dull, Dickensian way of telling stories. He mentions *David Copperfield*, which implies that not only is he well-read, but that he has no wish to make the reader sympathise with him, because he is not a helpless orphan who makes good in the end. Already, we are being led to infer that perhaps there is no happy ending to come.

Explore

What kind of character is David Copperfield? Why is Holden so anxious not to be compared to him?

Holden's attitude is cynical. He says that his parents are rather sensitive about family matters, and he is dismissive of his brother, a successful writer working in Hollywood. His attitude reveals his deep dislike for anything fake, and it is for this reason that he scorns his school which, in a solid and sensible way, claims to make its pupils model citizens – something he considers an entirely false claim.

Explore

Do you notice anything 'fake' about Holden in this chapter?

Pencey Preparatory School

Holden explains that his narrative will cover what happened to him the previous Christmas, before he had to rest and recuperate – we understand that he got into rather a run-down state, which may have led to some kind of mental breakdown. As the details of his school experience begin to unfold, we can understand how this may have come

Explore

Do you think that Holden always lives up to his high-minded principles?

about. Holden tells us that he was a student at Pencey Preparatory School in Agerstown, Pennsylvania, a good school with a long tradition and high academic standards.

The story begins on the afternoon of an important football game with a rival school. Holden, however, is not cheering with the rest of the boys, but sitting alone, away from the activities. He talks about Selma Thurmer, the headmaster's daughter, whom <u>he likes for her honesty, a quality Holden respects more than any other</u>.

A disastrous trip to New York

Holden fills us in on a disastrous outing to New York he has just returned from, as manager of the fencing team. A match with McBurney School had been arranged, but Holden leaves the foils on the subway. <u>He was ostracised by the entire team</u>, and for someone as sensitive as Holden, this would have been upsetting. Holden spends a few moments reflecting on his time at Pencey. He has trouble finding an appropriate memory and it is touching that the one he selects shows him as a regular teenager, playing with friends and not thinking too much.

At the end of the chapter he leaves to visit Mr Spencer, his old history teacher, in order to say goodbye.

Chapter 2

Holden visits the Spencers' home and immediately finds it <u>depressing</u>, with its strong reminders of illness and old age. Although we learn that Holden has respect for the caring Mr Spencer, he very soon begins to wish that he had not visited, as he is asked about his apparent <u>lack of purpose and interest in school</u>. Holden explains that he finds it very difficult to concentrate and illustrates this literally when he begins to think about the ducks in Central Park even while Mr Spencer is talking. He tells us that Mr Thurmer had compared life to a game and rejects this idea. We already know that Holden is rarely part of any sporting game, <u>preferring to be a loner rather than a team player</u>. Even when he is a member of a team (the fencing team), <u>he feels like an outsider</u>.

Holden fails his exams

We learn more about Holden's character when he explains that he thinks he has a poor vocabulary and that <u>he can be immature for his age</u>. Spencer grills Holden on his examination performance and reads one of Holden's answers to him, which is humorous because it is so bad. The fact that Holden believes it is acceptable to write his teacher a personal and inappropriate note, telling him not to feel bad about failing him, makes it even more amusing. On a more serious level, however, it is an indication of Holden's <u>lack of ability to communicate</u> in an appropriate way with older people and strangers – an idea developed later in the novel. Confronted with his academic failing, he becomes resentful. It seems that while he has no real problem with flunking school, <u>he is proud of his intelligence</u> and does not like to be embarrassed by his poor examination performance. Holden is forced to admit that he has already been expelled from several schools and uses the opportunity to defend his actions, in the face of such fake and phony characters.

Mr Spencer is genuinely worried for Holden's future

Mr Spencer tries to make Holden see that he must consider his future, but instead of making him see sense, it has the opposite effect. He resents Spencer's interference and leaves as soon as he is able to make an excuse. He is polite to Mr Spencer, but <u>leaves feeling quite depressed and sad</u>.

Chapter 3

Holden is proud that he is such an accomplished liar

Holden begins Chapter 3 by freely admitting that <u>he frequently</u>

lies and often for no real reason. He also explains how he lives in Ossenburger Memorial Wing of Pencey and, in a further example of his lack of faith in humanity, reveals how he believes that Ossenburger, a rich undertaker who gave his name to the wing, made his money burying people cheaply. This is another occasion when Holden shows his cynical view of adults and their motives, and he imagines Ossenburger praying to Jesus to kill a few more people off, so he can benefit from their large funeral expenses.

Robert Ackley is introduced

When Holden returns to his room, he tells us how he likes to read and discusses his favourite literature, showing that he is indeed a thoughtful and intelligent student. He enjoys being by himself and feels comfortable in the warm and cosy room. He puts on a red hunting hat he bought when he was in New York. Later, we are introduced to Robert Ackley, a fellow student whose room is connected to Holden's. Ackley is an unlikely companion, and Holden goes into great detail about his unlikeable personality, his scummy teeth and his bad complexion. At first Holden tries to ignore him, but Ackley is persistent and, clearly looking for company, insists on engaging him in conversation, all the while cutting his nails and leaving the clippings everywhere.

The handsome Stradlater

Holden also tells us about Stradlater, his roommate; a sporty, good-looking all-American student, who Ackley cannot stand, but who Holden defends, being able to see his good points, even though his description makes him seem a typical 'phony' student, concerned with looking good and showing off his body. Ironically, it is Ackley, not Holden, who has problems with Stradlater and hates his showing off and his conceited behaviour. At the end of the chapter Stradlater appears and, having a date waiting for him, decides to have a shave. Holden accompanies him.

Explore

Why do you think Holden defends Stradlater but refuses to defend Ackley?

Chapter 4

Idly killing time, Holden goes to the bathroom with Stradlater and chats to him while he gets ready for his date. Holden explains that, unlike him, his roommate is handsome in a typical yearbook fashion, and takes great pleasure in parading around showing off his good figure, even though his personal habits leave a little to be desired. This observation is interesting because it suggests that although his friend is good looking on the outside, deep down he is not so perfect. Bearing in mind Holden's view of people with double standards, it is surprising that he gets on well with Stradlater. Stradlater needs help with an English composition and asks Holden if he will write it for him while he goes out. Holden sees the irony of this, as he is flunking school, but agrees, as long as he has time.

Explore

If Holden is so anti falseness, why do you think he agrees to write the essay?

Holden's song and dance routine

In one of the lighter moments, Holden shows his whimsical side and begins tap-dancing across the bathroom floor, making Stradlater laugh. He also demonstrates his immaturity by grabbing him in a half-nelson, making him angry. Holden asks Stradlater about his date and is shocked when he finds out it is Jane Gallagher, a girl he used to live next door to. Although he keeps mentioning that he will go and say hello to her, he decides he is not in the mood. Holden asks Stradlater not to tell Jane he has been expelled and reminisces about her and the times they spent together. Stradlater leaves, borrowing Holden's jacket, having promised to pass on Holden's words. Ackley returns and, for once, Holden is pleased to see him because it stops him worrying about Stradlater and Jane on their date.

Chapter 5

A typical Saturday night

Holden explains that on Saturday evenings the students are given steak. He shows his cynicism again by thinking that this is a deliberate ploy by the school to impress the boys' parents. In fact, the meal is dry and virtually inedible. This is another example of people or things pretending to be something that they are not. After dinner, the boys go out into the snow and have fun.

As Holden does not have a date he decides to go to see a film with his friend Mal Brossard. Touchingly, he also invites Ackley as he knows that he will also be without a date, which demonstrates his <u>thoughtful, sensitive side</u>. In the end they decide to forego the film, as two of them have seen it, and have hamburgers instead.

Holden's brother Allie

After their evening, Ackley regales Holden with a story about a girl he has supposedly had sex with, but Holden knows he is lying because the story keeps changing. Perhaps because he is such a good liar himself, <u>he is good at spotting other people's falsehoods</u>. After a while he tells Ackley to leave so he can write Stradlater's essay for him. Holden cannot think of anything descriptive to write about, so he decides to describe his younger brother Allie's baseball mitt, which is covered in poems. In one of the most revealing passages in the novel, Holden explains how <u>his brother died of leukaemia</u> when he was only 11, and what a nice boy he was. When it happened, Holden locked himself in the family's garage and smashed every window, although he doesn't offer any explanation as to why he did this. The fact that he believes that such a personal subject as the mitt would be a good subject for an essay written for someone else, shows <u>Holden's strange sense of individuality</u>. He seems unable to understand why this would be an odd topic for an assignment and believes that as long as he does not use Allie's name it will be acceptable. He finishes the essay at 10.30 and spends some time alone, looking out of the window, listening to Ackley's snoring.

Chapter 6

In the dorm with Stradlater

In this chapter we have more evidence of Holden's mental turmoil, in this case his worry about Stradlater's date with Jane Gallagher. When his roommate returns, neither mentions the date at first, while Stradlater reads the essay Holden has written for him. He fails to appreciate Holden's efforts and is annoyed that he hasn't tackled the topic straightforwardly. He is only able to see one point of view and does not have the imagination to grasp that the essay is still valid, because it is so descriptive, even though it is about an object as apparently insignificant as a baseball glove. Holden's reaction is to tear up the essay.

Explore

Why is Holden so obsessed with Jane keeping all her kings in the back row?

Holden annoys Stradlater by smoking in the dorm. When Holden can bear the tension no longer, he asks about the date with Jane and is very nervous about the response. When he learns that all they did was sit in a borrowed car, he becomes even more distraught at the thought that Stradlater may have had sex with Jane; he even enquires about this, but receives no information.

Holden unsuccessfully attacks Stradlater, who retaliates by pinning him to the floor. Holden continues to call him a moron. He feels that Jane needs protecting. This is one example of Holden hanging on to the past; after all, he hasn't seen Jane for about 18 months, but still feels a close connection to her.

Text commentary

Since Holden will not keep quiet, he is floored again by Stradlater, but still maintains a barrage of insults until Stradlater goes to the bathroom. Before looking at the damage to his face, Holden puts on his hunting hat, with the peak to the back, as he likes it, and then goes through the shower to visit Ackley.

Chapter 7

Holden leaves Pencey Prep

Holden tries to interest Ackley in playing the card game canasta and asks if he can sleep in his roommate's empty bed. Although Ackley is not happy about this and is annoyed at being disturbed, he is still keen to know what the fight was about. Holden continues to be bothered by the thought of Stradlater and Jane in the car and gives an amusing account of Stradlater's seduction techniques.

Explore

Is Holden envious of Stradlater's sexual conquests? Why does he consider joining a monastery?

Ackley has fallen asleep, but since Holden is feeling so lonely and unhappy he wakes him to ask how you go about joining a monastery. He is not religious, but the life is appealing to him, perhaps because it would avoid the pressures of outside life and relationships. It would be a way of putting his life on hold.

Since it is making him too miserable, Holden decides to leave Pencey straight away and to stay in a hotel in New York for a few days. He feels he cannot go home until his parents have digested the news of his expulsion. He is nearly crying when he is ready to go, so puts on his hunting hat and yells defiantly, calling everyone a moron. However, even leaving with a flourish backfires, because he almost trips over peanut shells on the way out.

Quick questions

1   *What is the name of Holden's school?*

2   *Why has Holden been expelled?*

3   *What has Holden bought in New York that day?*

4   *Who visits Holden's room by walking through the connecting shower?*

5   *What does Holden write about in Stradlater's essay?*

A process of elimination

1   *The story starts on a Saturday in Spring/Summer/Winter.*

2   *Holden watches the football game from the stands/his dorm window/the top of a hill.*

3   *Holden is manager of the football/fencing/ice hockey team.*

4   *His team members are annoyed with him because he has lost the equipment/the train tickets/the map.*

5   *Holden says goodbye to the headmaster/history teacher/PE teacher.*

Who does this?

1   *Who says nothing to Holden on the train from New York?*

2   *Who wants to put some sense into Holden's head?*

3   *Who tells Holden that he always does everything back to front?*

4   *Who complains that people never believe what you say?*

5   *Who swears and blasphemes a great deal?*

Establishing Holden's character

1   *What sort of people does Holden most dislike?*

2   *How does he like to wear his hunting hat?*

3   *How does he react when his brother Allie dies?*

4   *What does he most dislike about Ackley?*

5   *What state does he say his nerves are in?*

Chapters 8 to 14

Chapter 8

On the train to New York

Explore

Why does Holden always tell us exactly what he does with his hat?

Holden goes by rail to New York, the main setting of the novel. His only significant action is removing his hunting hat and putting it in his pocket.

When a new passenger sits next to Holden she notices the Pencey Prep sticker on his case, so strikes up a conversation, since her son, Ernest Morrow, goes to the school. Probably because Holden considers Ernest to be one of the most despicable characters in the school's history, he begins a series of lies to Mrs Morrow, starting by claiming to be Rudolf Schmidt, the dorm janitor (caretaker). Holden likes women and he finds Mrs Morrow attractive, which might partly explain why he invents many complimentary points about the insensitive Ernest. He also tries to act in what he sees as a sophisticated, grown-up manner, by offering her a cigarette and a cocktail. When she wonders why 'Rudolf' has left school early, Holden digs deeper into lies by pretending that he has to have an operation for a brain tumour. He tries to extricate himself from the conversation, admitting to the reader that his lies can go on for hours once he starts, but he has to lie again to avoid accepting an invitation to visit the Morrows in the summer.

Explore

Research a map of the USA and trace Holden's route from school to New York City.

Chapter 9

Holden books into a hotel

Holden arrives in New York and immediately goes to a public phone booth to get in touch with someone, but he

Text commentary

cannot think of anyone to call. He takes a taxi to the Edmont Hotel and asks the driver if he knows where the ducks from Central Park go in winter, when the lake is frozen. The driver thinks that Holden is making fun of him. He wears his hunting hat in the cab, but removes it before checking into the hotel, so that he gives the right impression.

The only view from his window is across to the other side of the shabby hotel, where he watches other guests. He is fascinated, which leads him to consider his attitude to sex – something that he freely admits that he does not understand. He phones a stripper, Faith Cavendish, whose details a slight acquaintance had given him. They have an unsatisfactory conversation, during which Faith suspects that Holden might be very young. She makes excuses not to meet that evening and he does not take up her invitation to have a drink the next day. This is the first of a series of unsuccessful attempts at connecting with others in New York.

Chapter 10

In the Lavender Room night club

While getting ready to go down to the hotel's night club, Holden thinks about his young sister, Phoebe. He feels like talking to her, because of her sense and understanding, but cannot risk it because his parents would be bound to answer the phone. He is by far the youngest in the club and fails to persuade the waiter to serve him with alcohol, for which he needs to be 21. He tries to strike up a conversation with three women from out of town on the next table. He considers them stupid, but manages to persuade them to dance with him in turn. They are happy for him to buy them drinks all evening, but they laugh at him and make fun of his age, and are only interested in spotting movie stars. Holden is clearly out of his depth and not nearly as grown up as he likes to think he is. He stays in the club until it closes.

Chapter 11

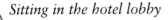

Sitting in the hotel lobby

Holden sits in the lobby after leaving the club, because he cannot stop thinking about Jane Gallagher. He uses baseball imagery to describe how far Jane would have permitted Stradlater to go with her, but this time it is not just their date that preys on his mind. He also thinks about how he met Jane when they were neighbours one summer holiday 18 months ago, what they did together and how close they were, although that relationship is not physical. Jane is the only non-family member who has ever seen Allie's baseball mitt, showing Holden's high opinion of her. He gives a very detailed description of their time together, when they played golf, tennis and checkers.

Holden decides to go to Ernie's night club in Greenwich Village, a place D.B. has taken him a number of times.

Explore

What use does Salinger make of the motif of games and sport in the novel? Which games and sports are mentioned?

Chapter 12

Ernie's night club, Greenwich Village

In a cab, on the way to Ernie's, Holden feels lonely and depressed by New York at night. In an attempt to strike up a conversation, he asks the driver, whose name is Horwitz, about the ducks in Central Park. Horwitz becomes very impatient with him, thinking it a stupid question. He introduces the topic of fish, to explain to Holden that they survive satisfactorily all winter; Mother Nature doesn't just let them die. Holden offers to buy Horwitz a drink, which he refuses. Holden comments on Horwitz's touchiness, not realising how annoying he can be when his questioning is so persistent.

In the crowded club, Holden has to wait for a table. While doing so, he considers how phony Ernie has become, partly because he has received too much adulation from his audience. When he is eventually seated, Holden watches his neighbours with amusement. Through the waiter, he tries to ask Ernie to join him for a drink, but suspects that his message has not been passed on.

Explore

Why does Holden ask Ernie to join him? Does this make him a phony too?

Lillian Simmons, an ex-girlfriend of D.B.'s, comes up to him with her naval officer date. Holden considers them both to be <u>supremely</u> <u>phony</u>. Lillian wants him to join them at their table, but he makes the excuse that he is meeting someone elsewhere, so has no choice but to leave.

Chapter 13

An encounter in Holden's hotel room

Holden does not feel like getting another cab, so he walks the long distance back to the hotel. The hunting hat, with its ear flaps, proves very useful against the biting cold. He regrets that someone at Pencey has stolen his gloves and that he is incapable of acting aggressively and bravely towards such people, mainly because <u>he dislikes face-to-face fist fights</u>. This introspection makes him more depressed.

Explore

Gloves and hands feature frequently in the text. What do you think the significance of this might be?

In the elevator up to his room, the lift boy, Maurice, asks Holden if he would like a girl to visit him. He agrees, on impulse, but thinks that it might be useful practice, since he is still a virgin. When the young prostitute, Sunny, arrives, Holden is unsettled when she removes her dress. He suggests they talk for a while, but the girl is impatient and has no conversation. Holden tells her that he will still pay her, but that <u>he does not feel like having sex that night</u>, because he has just had a serious operation on his spine. They have a disagreement

Explore

Where else does Holden make false claims about an operation? Why does he do this?

about the fee, because Sunny demands double the amount agreed with Maurice.

Chapter 14

A fight in Holden's room

Holden feels increasingly miserable, so he thinks about Allie and talks aloud to him, which is something he does when he is depressed. Eventually he goes to bed and tries unsuccessfully to pray. He dislikes the Disciples, because he feels they let Jesus down. It is significant that the character he does relate to in the Bible is a martyr-like follower who lacerates himself. This is redolent of his admiration for Mercutio in *Romeo and Juliet* – another character who dies for his beliefs. Holden is certainly drawn to anyone who is prepared to make sacrifices for a nobler cause.

Explore

Does Holden feel let down by people?

Maurice knocks on the door, wanting the money he claims is owed to Sunny. Holden argues the case, but Maurice pushes Holden out of the way and comes into the room with Sunny. He intimidates Holden, but rather than giving in, which would have been the sensible course of action, Holden tries to persuade them to leave empty handed. He describes the scene with some humour, emphasising that it might all have been different if he wasn't dressed in his pyjamas. When Sunny takes five dollars out of his wallet, Holden breaks down in tears. This has some effect on the girl and she tries to persuade Maurice to leave Holden alone now that they have the money, but he still taunts him. Holden retaliates, as he had to Stradlater, by calling him a moron, which results in him being punched to the floor. After Maurice and Sunny have left, Holden staggers to the bathroom, acting out a film scene as if he has been shot, despite despising the movies. He later goes to bed, saying he is feeling suicidal.

Text commentary

Quick quiz 2

Quick questions

1   Who does Holden talk to on the train to New York?

2   Which board game did Holden play with Jane Gallagher?

3   Who arranges for Holden to meet Sunny, the prostitute?

4   How old is Holden at the time he is writing about?

A process of elimination

1   Holden arrives at Penn/Grand Central/Broadway Station.

2   His first outing in New York is to the Lavender Room/Radio City/Ernie's club.

3   Holden sits in his room/the park/the hotel lobby and thinks about Jane Gallagher.

4   Holden first met Jane Gallagher in New York/Maine/Agerstown?

5   Maurice punches Holden because he owed money/insulted Sunny/called him a moron.

Who does this?

1   Who wonders if Holden is old enough to order a drink on the train?

2   Who thinks that Holden is making fun of him when he asks strange questions?

3   Who tells Holden that he sounds a little young, but attractive, on the phone?

4   Who lets Holden dance with them and buy them several drinks?

5   Who takes five bucks out of Holden's wallet?

Impressions of Holden

1   What does Holden say about his habit of lying?

2   What is Holden's favourite word to describe the adult world?

3   How does Holden try to appear adult in bars?

4   Who does Holden talk to when he feels very depressed?

5   How does Holden act when Maurice has gone, after he is punched in the stomach?

Chapters 15 to 20

Chapter 15

Breakfast with nuns in the Grand Central Station

After a short sleep, Holden phones Sally Hayes, an old girlfriend. He is not very keen on her, because <u>he considers her to be phony and unintelligent</u>, but he thinks she is good-looking.

Holden takes a cab to Grand Central Station. He could not risk ordering breakfast at the hotel in case Maurice was the one to deliver it. He talks to two nuns and gives them money for charity. Interestingly, it is exactly the same amount – ten dollars – that he gave to the prostitute, but in this case he parts with it more than willingly. With one nun, Holden discusses texts he has read, particularly *Romeo and Juliet*. <u>Holden does not consider the nuns to be phonies</u> and enjoys talking to them. By mistake he blows smoke in their faces as he says goodbye to them, which worries him, because of <u>his respect for them</u>.

Explore

Why does the character of Mercutio appeal most to Holden?

Chapter 16

Broadway and Central Park

We see Holden in two contrasting locations in this chapter, which bring out very different feelings in him. First he walks towards Broadway, a bustling commercial and theatre area, where he hopes to buy a record called *Little Shirley Beans* for Phoebe. On the way he thinks about the nuns. He likes the fact that they don't go anywhere smart or pretentious, but he also feels sad that they do not have the opportunity to do so. <u>Holden finds Broadway claustrophobic</u>. He sees a mother, father and young son walking home from church. The boy makes a particular impression on Holden. He keeps carefully in a straight line and sings a song, which Holden hears as 'If a body catch a body coming through the rye'. The child is behaving spontaneously and makes Holden feel less depressed.

In spite of the crowds Holden manages to buy the record quickly, which improves his mood further, and he looks forward to finding Phoebe in the park to give it to her. First he tries to phone Jane Gallagher, but hangs up when her mother answers the phone. He buys tickets for a show starring America's most famous and skilful acting couple, the Lunts. Holden finds most actors phony, but knows that Sally will be thrilled.

Holden takes a cab to the park and looks for Phoebe in the area where she normally skates. He cannot see her, so asks a young girl getting ready to skate. She doesn't know where Phoebe is, but Holden helps her to tie her skates and is so impressed with her niceness and politeness that he offers to buy her a drink, which she declines. He walks across the park to the Museum of Natural History, intending to look round. He loved the museum as a child and feels nostalgic about it. He likes the way that nothing changes in there, even though the visitor himself will have changed between each visit. He puts his hunting hat on at this stage, as if to protect himself from thoughts of growing up. He thinks about how Phoebe also changes each time she looks at the exhibits, which makes him feel sad. He feels that some things should always stay the same. When he reaches the museum he no longer wants to go in, so reluctantly catches a cab to the Biltmore Hotel, where he is due to meet Sally.

Chapter 17

On the date with Sally Hayes

While waiting for Sally in the lobby, Holden watches girls and considers how their lives will develop. He is struck by how stunning

Sally looks, which compensates for her being late and him not liking her very much. He even thinks he's in love with her and would like to marry her. Holden is not very interested in the play they watch. He thinks the stars act convincingly, but considers that doing something too well can lead to showing off. The interval gives him the opportunity to observe many phony people, particularly an acquaintance of Sally's who monopolises Sally during this and the next interval. By the time they leave the show, Holden is aggravated by Sally. He would have taken her straight home, but she suggests ice skating at Radio City.

The skating outing is a disaster. Neither Holden nor Sally can skate properly, though Sally looks the part – and knows it – in her short skating skirt. They retreat to the bar, where Holden's confused state intensifies and he is unable to engage her in a proper, interesting conversation. While Sally is down to earth and unimaginative, wanting to know whether Holden is going to help her with the ritual of decorating the Christmas tree, Holden wants to have a deep conversation about life. He tells her what he hates about New York and boys' boarding schools. He admits that he is in bad shape, and suddenly suggests to Sally that they run off together up to the northern states of Massachusetts and Vermont and live simply in a cabin. Sally tries to reason with him, telling him his plan is just a fantasy, and that they should wait until they are older. Holden, however, wants to seize the moment while they are young because it will all be different when he has joined the adult world, which he thinks is full of phonies.

Explore

Why is Holden so keen to grab this opportunity with Sally? Taking an opportunity in this way is called *carpe diem* which means 'seize the day'.

Holden is becoming depressed and more unstable, as is shown by his alternating between being very noisy and very quiet. The conversation comes to a head when Sally replies to Holden's comments that she probably doesn't know what he's talking about by saying that he does not either, which leads to him insulting her. Sally is furious and upset and refuses to accept both Holden's apologies and

Text commentary

his offers to take her home. Holden's mental turmoil is illustrated by his laughing loudly, despite her distress. In the end he leaves, which would have been considered very ungentlemanly behaviour in the 1940s. Holden's confusion is shown further when he admits he has no idea why he asked Sally to go away with him, although he meant it at the moment of asking.

Chapter 18

After the disastrous date with Sally, Holden decides to call Jane after he has got himself something to eat. His choice, a simple cheese sandwich and glass of malted milk, reminds us of his youth. It is a wholesome snack and perhaps suggests Holden's desire to be both young and back home again. His decision to call Jane also seems to be a yearning for a better past. (Certainly he has already forgotten proposing to Sally!) He then remembers how Jane danced with Al Pike from Choate, a character who sounds rather like Stradlater. Despite Holden's misgivings about his arrogance, Jane thought that Al had an inferiority complex and felt sorry for him. Holden believes that girls divide boys into two distinct types, either conceited or insecure. The girl's decision does not seem to depend on what the boy's personality actually is, but whether or not the girl likes him and what impression he manages to create. This is another example of Holden's frustration with not being understood, and society's general inability to judge people correctly. Although Holden wants to speak to Jane again, he can't because no one seems to be at home. Eventually he decides to call Carl Luce, a friend who went to Whooton School with him and for whom Holden has great admiration, because he is so intelligent.

Explore

Why do you think that Holden chooses this moment to call Jane again?

Radio City Music Hall

In order to pass the time until his meeting with Carl, Holden goes to see a film at Radio City Music Hall, but gets very irritated with a woman who sits next to him. She gets very emotional during the sentimental film, but will not let her child go to the toilet. Holden sees this as an act of hypocrisy – someone who claims to be sensitive, but cannot even deal with their own child when he is in need.

Explore

Research this influential writer and director. Why do you think that Holden admires him?

Holden describes the film, which reminds him of D.B.'s experience in the war. His brother hated the army, but encouraged Holden to read *A Farewell to Arms*, by Ernest Hemingway, which Holden believes celebrates soldiers. He can't understand how D.B. could like this book and also like the writer Ring Lardner.

Explore

Widen your reading by getting to know the works of other authors, such as *A Farewell to Arms* by Ernest Hemingway.

Holden is emphatic in his dislike of the military, and it seems that it is as much the notion of teamwork that offends him as the notion of violence. He even quotes an occasion when he joined the Scouts and hated looking at the neck of the boy in front. His sense of individuality means that he is opposed to anything that is likely to bond people together. He declares that if there is a war he would refuse to take part and is even glad for the new invention of nuclear weapons, for he would volunteer to sit right on top of a bomb, rather than fight for his country. It is typical of Holden that his views can be very lucid and intelligent one moment, then dashed with a very childish remark the next moment.

Chapter 19

Holden meets Carl at the Wicker Bar, an expensive and flash bar in the Seton Hotel. He arrives early because he has nothing else to do and orders a few whiskey and sodas, even though he is under age. Despite being so against people who pretend, it seems that, in a typical teenage fashion, Holden has no problems at all pretending to be older than he is in order to try and buy alcohol! While he is waiting he examines the bar and muses on how false everyone seems. He notices that many of the men look as if they might be homosexual – possibly because they are all dressed up – and he remembers how his friend Carl was an 'expert' at spotting such people, particularly Hollywood actors who were supposed to be the epitome of manliness. With irony, he mentions that, in fact, he always suspected his friend Carl to be a homosexual. This chapter is significant because it reveals much about <u>Holden's</u> <u>confused</u> <u>sense</u> of <u>identity</u> <u>and</u> <u>his</u> <u>muddled</u> <u>sexual</u> <u>emotions</u>. On one hand, he claims to be open-minded and lacking in the hypocrisy that he sees everywhere, and yet on the other, he proves himself to be a typical prejudiced teenage lad, obsessed with other people's sexual encounters.

A conversation with Carl Luce

When Carl arrives he appears older than Holden and is irritated at Holden's apparent immaturity, especially when he starts grilling Carl about his sex life. Holden is fascinated when Carl admits that he is seeing an Oriental sculptress, who is much older than him. It is interesting that Carl is one of the few people who impresses Holden, partly because of his intelligence, but also because of his 'worldliness'. Certainly <u>Holden</u> <u>reveals</u> <u>his</u> <u>lack</u> <u>of</u> <u>experience</u> with the barrage of very personal questions that he asks his friend, and admits that he has trouble forming any kind of physical relationship with girls. He confesses that unless he really likes the girl he cannot feel desire. This would seem to be a wise thing in a boy who is growing up, however, we know that <u>Holden</u> <u>finds</u> <u>it</u> <u>difficult</u> <u>to</u> <u>communicate</u> <u>with</u> <u>girls</u> and, therefore, his chances of being able to identify with someone else enough to get to know them and like them seem remote.

We are left with a sad picture of a teenage boy frustrated by his lack of sexual success and only gaining excitement vicariously, through the stories of others.

Holden's reaction to Carl's suggestion of psychoanalysis

Carl reminds Holden that he previously suggested he undertake some kind of therapy, and Holden remains silent. (After such a devastating loss as his younger brother dying, and Holden's apparent emotional issues, it would seem to the reader that this is probably exactly what Holden needs and clearly should have had some time ago.) Holden is pensive and interested enough to inquire further from Carl what the therapy would entail. Carl, however, appears to have lost interest by this stage and tells Holden he needs to leave. In a poignant moment Holden begs his friend to stay for one more drink because he is so lonely, but Carl has run out of time.

Explore

What is the purpose of 'therapy'? Why do you think Carl suggests this for Holden?

Chapter 20

A drunken phone call

After Carl leaves, Holden remains in the bar by himself, drinking until he is less than rational. In this drunken state he decides that it would be a good time to call Jane. However, as on other occasions during the course of the novel, Holden is still unable to bring himself to make contact with her. Instead, even though he is extremely drunk, he calls Sally. Because of his drunken state, when Sally's grandmother answers the phone and tells Holden that Sally is asleep, he becomes quite belligerent and demands to speak with her. Eventually Sally speaks with Holden and asks him to call her the next day.

Since he has no one to talk to, he decides to leave, and begins crying because he is so lonely. He is helped by a hat-check girl, who is worried about him and makes him put his hat on before he goes outside in the cold weather.

After leaving the Wicker Bar, Holden realises he has run out of money and so walks to Central Park to try and find the elusive ducks. On the way he stumbles and drops Phoebe's record, which smashes into small pieces. He is devastated: <u>the record symbolises the link he has with his sister</u> and also the comforts of home. He picks up the pieces, even though he knows they are useless. At his most cold and miserable he finds an empty park bench and sits there in the dark, after failing to find his ducks. He is on the verge of having a complete breakdown, and begins to imagine what would happen if he were to die. Morbidly, he imagines his own funeral and takes comfort from the fact that his parents would not allow Phoebe to attend. This is very interesting. Holden was not permitted to attend Allie's funeral, and it is possible that this is one of the reasons why he has never had a sense of finality in the relationship with his brother. He does not see that perhaps Phoebe might need to say a formal goodbye to her brother, should something fatal happen to him. Touchingly, he recalls visiting his brother's grave and getting upset that Allie should be in the damp earth, while he was warm and dry. His thoughts of Phoebe, however, lead him to decide to visit her, just in case she should not see him again. He is so depressed, <u>he realises that he needs to communicate with someone who understands him</u>. These thoughts of death suggest that perhaps Holden's over-active imagination might really lead him to consider suicide.

Quick questions

1 Which Shakespeare play does Holden discuss with the nun?

2 Which character from this play does Holden most like?

3 What does Holden buy for Phoebe?

4 Where does Holden hope to find Phoebe, so that he can give her the present?

5 How does Holden help the girl in the park?

A process of elimination

1 Holden has breakfast in his hotel room/the lobby/Grand Central Station.

2 Holden hates it if someone has cheap suitcases/cheap ice skates/cheap clothes.

3 When Holden first sees Sally he wants to escape/marry her/phone Jane.

4 Holden takes Sally roller skating/ice skating/dancing.

5 Carl Luce is an old friend from Pencey Prep/Elkton Hills/Whooton School.

Who does this?

1 Who sits next to Holden in the station?

2 Who sings Comin' Through the Rye?

3 Who suggests Phoebe might be in the museum?

4 Who refuses to accept Holden's apologies?

5 Who tells Holden he is annoying because of his constant questions about sex?

Holden in New York

1 What makes Holden look individual as he walks through the city?

2 Why does hearing the song make Holden feel less depressed?

3 Why is Holden longing to get out of Broadway?

4 What does Holden tell Sally that he feels about living in New York?

5 Why does Holden decide to go home to see Phoebe?

Chapters 21 to 26

Chapter 21

A private moment with Phoebe

Holden returns home and sneaks in, so that he does not wake up his parents. He lies again when he pretends to the elevator boy that he has a bad leg. We learn that Holden's mother is very nervous and has trouble sleeping, so she spends most of her time smoking cigarettes – like Holden. We imagine that this may be another result of Allie's sudden death.

Holden finds Phoebe asleep in D.B.'s room and he idly glances through her notebooks, noticing that she has been doodling and writing notes during lessons. Phoebe can do no wrong in his eyes and he is tolerant of her idiosyncrasies in a way that he is not about any other character in the novel. He looks at her in a sentimental way while she is asleep, and he feels a wave of love for his sister.

Explore

Phoebe keeps changing her name in her notebook. Holden also gives false names. Why do you think they do this?

Phoebe is angry with Holden

Holden wakes Phoebe, who is very pleased to see her brother and hugs him. She tells him that she is in a play at school and that their parents are at a party. Holden shows Phoebe the broken pieces of the record, which she touchingly saves by putting them safely in the drawer of her bedside table. She excitedly tells her brother about a boy at school she has been teasing because he keeps following her, and Holden explains that it is probably because he likes her and is too young to tell her. Phoebe forces Holden to explain that he has been expelled and she guesses that their parents will be furious. Holden tries to put her reaction down to over-exaggeration, but she is right. Even at ten years old she understands the implications of Holden's situation and demonstrates that <u>she</u> <u>is</u> <u>really</u> <u>much</u> <u>more</u> <u>grown</u> <u>up</u> <u>than</u> <u>her</u> <u>older</u> <u>brother</u>. To express her frustration and anger with him she covers her head with a pillow and refuses to talk to him any more.

Chapter 22

After Phoebe calms down, Holden explains that <u>he</u> <u>could</u> <u>not</u> <u>stand</u> <u>the</u> <u>number</u> <u>of</u> <u>people</u> <u>who</u> <u>were</u> <u>fake</u> <u>and</u> <u>hypocritical</u> at Pencey. He tells her about how Robert Ackley was ostracised and uses this as an example of how 'phony' most of the pupils were (conveniently forgetting how irritating he found Ackley himself). Interestingly, he tells her about a secret fraternity that he did not want to join, but was too cowardly not to. This tells us a great deal about Holden and his desire to be an individual. Even though he is against societies and teams, <u>he</u> <u>does</u> <u>not</u> <u>have</u> <u>the</u> <u>moral</u> <u>fibre</u> <u>to</u> <u>remain</u> <u>independent</u>. He is too 'yellow'.

Explore

Why is 1776, mentioned by Holden, such a significant date for Americans?

Holden talks about Mr Spencer and we realise how much he genuinely liked and admired his teacher. Holden does not appreciate that school days are, for some, a positive experience, and can be looked back on in a sentimental way.

The sad story of James Castle

Phoebe is exasperated and perceptively informs him that he does not like anything, so he tells her about a boy at Elkton Hills called James Castle. This boy was being bullied and retaliated by saying something negative about one of his attackers, called Phil Stabile. James was a weak and frail pupil, but even when Phil and six friends began to demand he take back his words he refused. The bullies tried to intimidate him, but instead of losing his integrity and backing down James jumped out of the dormitory window and plunged to his death.

This memory is important to Holden because it reinforces his view about honesty in the face of adversity. The bullies conform to everything Holden hates about American schools, and James becomes a kind of hero to him – a character who is physically weaker but has great moral strength. This is what Holden himself aspires to, but the fact that he cannot stop himself lying suggests that he has some way to go. His admiration for James also suggests that Holden sees death as a noble action and perhaps hints again that he is beginning to have suicidal thoughts of his own.

The catcher in the rye

Phoebe inquires whether Holden likes anything and he tells her he likes Allie. His sister reminds him that Allie is dead, but Holden says that does not matter. This exchange illustrates how much Holden is still suffering over his younger brother's death. He tells Phoebe that what he would most like to be is a catcher in a field of rye, waiting to save children from falling off a cliff. This is a touching picture, and typical of Holden, in as much as it contains an idealised scene from childhood, with young children happily and innocently playing. In an egotistical way, he plays the role of the hero, protecting them from harm. The fact that he is not part of the scene, but distanced from it, is also significant. He knows that he has left his own childhood behind. What makes this ambition especially unusual, however, is that it has a surreal quality, and indicates that Holden is becoming increasingly detached from what is considered acceptable behaviour. He randomly decides to call Mr Antolini, an old English teacher.

Explore

The Kevin Costner baseball film, *Field of Dreams*, has many parallels with *The Catcher in the Rye*. What ideas do they share?

Chapter 23

Holden phones Mr Antolini, even though it is very late. Mr Antolini, almost expecting something to have happened, asks Holden if he is alright, and he explains that he has been expelled. His old teacher tells him to come over if he wants to. This seemingly random call is put into context when Holden explains that Mr Antolini was the teacher who finally picked up the broken body of James Castle. It suggests that Holden sees himself in a similar position to James and is <u>making a distress call to the only person he knows who might save him</u>.

Holden and Phoebe dance together

After making his telephone call Holden goes back to see Phoebe and, in a touching, shared moment, they dance together. This shows his <u>need for some kind of physical comfort and closeness with another person</u>, a person he can really talk to. The two of them are disturbed by the return of their parents, and Holden's mother questions Phoebe about the smell of cigarettes. She hides the fact that Holden has returned and takes the blame herself. Holden asks Phoebe to lend him money, but then feels bad when she gives him her Christmas present money. Holden begins to cry and <u>in a real sign of emotional breakdown</u> he is unable to stop. Eventually <u>he gives Phoebe his prized red hunting hat</u>, one of the few possessions he treasures, and leaves. This is an ominous moment, revealing Holden's fragile emotional state. His parting gift to Phoebe suggests that this is a farewell token, and that he may never see her again.

Explore

Why does Holden go to such lengths to hide from his parents?

Chapter 24

The Antolinis' apartment

Holden catches a taxi to the Antolinis' apartment, even though he can hardly spare the money, but <u>he is so physically weak and sick</u> that he has no choice. He tells us that Mr Antolini and his wife are both intellectuals. When he arrives his old teacher answers the door, drinking a cocktail and wearing a bathrobe. He explains that they have just had a party and offers

Holden a cigarette. Perhaps he is aware of Holden nervous disposition, which would make him turn to smoking.

Holden and his old teacher discuss Pencey, which makes Holden feel increasingly dizzy and sick. Although he seems unrepentant at being expelled from his school, he is almost <u>physically unprepared</u> <u>to</u> <u>take</u> <u>the</u> <u>consequences</u> <u>of</u> <u>his</u> <u>actions</u>. He had a similar reaction when he was forced to face the truth of the situation by Mr Spencer, Carl Luce and Phoebe. Holden tells Mr Antolini about another boy at school who was picked on for being weak at a particular subject. In the same way that he admired James Castle for holding on to his principles, Holden feels great sympathy for Richard Kinsella, who almost failed his debate class because he was nervous and kept digressing. <u>Holden</u> <u>naturally</u> <u>feels</u> <u>an</u> <u>affinity</u> <u>with</u> <u>the</u> <u>underdog</u>.

> **❝The mark of the immature man is that he wants to die nobly for a cause, while the mark of the mature man is that he wants to live humbly for one. ❞**

Mr Antolini informs Holden that he recently had lunch with Holden's father, and gently tries to tell him that he is heading for a fall. He tells Holden that he is in danger of hating everything, but Holden replies that even when he hates people, after a while he misses them.

Mr Antolini tries to explain that the kind of fall he means is an emotional breakdown, where there is little chance of recovery. He quotes the words of a psychoanalyst called Willhelm Stekel, who believed that it was the mark of a better man if he could live through his trauma, rather than giving in and dying as a martyr. These words are of great importance for they show that <u>Mr</u> <u>Antolini</u> <u>knows</u> <u>full</u> <u>well</u> <u>that</u> <u>Holden</u> <u>is</u> <u>in</u> <u>an</u> <u>extremely</u> <u>fragile</u> <u>state</u> and may be considering suicide. It also shows that he understands how Holden views death as a noble, worthwhile venture, and is trying, in a subtle way, to prove to him that this is not so. Unfortunately, Holden is beyond help and does not see the significance of these words.

Mr Antolini encourages Holden to try and find some kind of peace and contentment with himself and be able to offer something truly worthwhile to the world. Overcome with tiredness, Holden simply agrees. Mr Antolini arranges the couch for Holden to sleep on and asks him about Sally and Jane. Holden briefly mentions his date with Sally and then explains that he will be calling Jane the next day. His desire to speak with Jane is still strong, and we hope that by the end of the novel, Holden will have achieved at least this one small ambition.

Holden feels betrayed and leaves in a panic

Holden falls asleep and wakes up to find Mr Antolini sitting beside him, gently patting his head. In alarm he jumps up and demands to know what Mr Antolini is doing. Suspicious of his teacher's intentions, Holden explains that he needs to collect his bag from the station. In a hurry he dresses and leaves, promising to return. This is one of the pivotal moments in the text for it shows Holden, once again, at a point of possible redemption which he then runs from. We know that he is in a fragile, emotional state and with his confused ideas about sexual relationships it is wholly possible that his conclusion about Mr Antolini is entirely wrong. Given the conversation they had just had, and knowing how much he understands Holden's position, and cares for him, it seems much more likely that Mr Antolini's actions are driven by empathy. Feeling a paternal concern for him, gently patting him on the head might have been his way of showing real concern for the boy, rather than any homosexual advance.

Holden, however, feels deeply betrayed by someone he viewed as a kind of hero of the helpless. In reality, it just gives him another excuse to run from someone who is trying to make him face his future. Nevertheless, it is an ambiguous moment, and we are left to decide for ourselves what Mr Antolini's motivation might have been.

Chapter 25

After leaving the Antolinis', Holden walks to Grand Central Station. He collects his bags and sleeps rough on one of the benches. He reflects on Mr Antolini and, perhaps beginning to think more lucidly, begins to regret not going back to the apartment. Picking up a magazine in the station, Holden begins to read an article about hormones and cancer, and in his morbid and hyper-sensitive state <u>worries about whether he has a terminal disease</u>.

Holden is saved by Allie

As he walks up Fifth Avenue, Holden plays a mental game with himself, imagining that every time he steps off of a curb he will fall down for eternity. This parallels Mr Antolini's words about heading for a fall. Holden is literally acting out Mr Antolini's prophetic, but metaphoric, words. To make himself feel better <u>he imagines that he is with Allie</u> and begs his little brother not to let him disappear. This is a very poignant moment, for <u>we truly see how much Allie still means to Holden</u>. In his eyes his brother is the one who can save him from his future. It indicates that Holden is not ready to die just yet, and needs the thought of Allie to keep him going.

Holden makes a decision to run away, preferring to be left alone and not bothered by anyone. He intends never to go to school again but be content with a menial job, pretending to be a deaf-mute so he will not have to talk to anyone. In this way he feels <u>he will be protected from falseness, hypocrisy</u> and all the things that he cannot bear.

He decides to see Phoebe at school to say goodbye. At the school he becomes enraged and obsessed by some graffiti and wipes it away. This attempt to protect the younger children from something bad symbolises his 'Catcher in the Rye' dream. All he wants is to save small children, but in reality he is not in a position to rescue anyone, not even himself, against the harshness of the adult world.

The trip to the zoo and the carousel ride

Holden writes Phoebe a note, asking her to meet him at the museum, so he can return her money. He walks to the museum and, after needing the toilet, loses consciousness, probably through lack of food, no sleep and stress. He says that when he comes to he feels better, but we realise that he really is on his last legs, and his journey must surely be nearing an end. His physical state now reflects his lack of mental well-being.

After chatting to two young children about Egyptians he sees Phoebe, touchingly wearing Holden's hat and dragging a huge suitcase. Knowing that Holden is going to run away, she asks if she can go with him. Holden loses his temper with her and tells her she can't go with him, and she begins to cry. She throws Holden's hunting hat at him and although he is upset he says nothing, but puts it in his pocket. Phoebe refuses to return to school, despite Holden offering to walk her back, so he persuades her to take a walk with him to the zoo.

Explore

Do you think the zoo has any greater significance in the novel than just being a place to visit?

The zoo is quiet and Holden buys Phoebe a ticket for the carousel and watches her go round and round. It is another touching moment between brother and sister and embodies Holden's idealised view of childhood. It also symbolises his own personal struggle, where things go round and round but never change or lead anywhere. Holden is physically and mentally unable to break free of the circle in which he finds himself. He is not strong enough, despite believing that he is morally stronger than others. In a show of forgiveness, Phoebe kisses Holden. It begins to rain and, watching Phoebe have fun on the merry-go-round, Holden finds himself crying in the rain. He tells Phoebe he will go home. Significantly, Phoebe puts his hunting hat on him and Holden admits that in the torrential rain it gives him a little protection. As the hat is such a powerful metaphor for

Explore

What do you think prompts Holden's sudden change of plan?

individuality and comfort, it suggests that Phoebe has given Holden just enough reason to face the difficulties of growing up.

Chapter 26

The narrative concludes

Holden abruptly ends his story here, refusing to explain what happened when he returned home, but he does indicate that he got very 'sick'. He is seeing a psychoanalyst who is forcing him to address questions about his future, but he is still unable to answer them. He is forging a closer relationship with his older brother, D.B., who visits him often, and he says he often misses his old friends from Pencey – even Ackley. His final words to the readers take the form of advice. He tells us not to confide in anyone, because as soon as we do we will start to miss them. This is extremely poignant for it shows that Holden now realises the importance of communication. He understands that by opening up to people, you build relationships. He currently believes this is a bad thing because it leaves you vulnerable. In a way this is true, but we hope Holden realises, in time, that it can be a very positive thing also. The ending is ambiguous for we have no real hint that Holden will recover and begin to see the world more positively. The novel ends almost in a cyclical fashion, with Holden referring to the same characters he talked about in the opening chapters. He certainly still seems suspicious and cynical, but as readers, we hope he will be able to get off his own self-destructive carousel.

Explore

What do you think will happen to Holden? Do we have any clues about his future?

Text commentary

Quick questions

1   What does Phoebe do with the broken record?

2   Who wrote Comin' Through the Rye?

3   Who tells Holden the correct words to the song?

4   What does Holden give Phoebe as he leaves?

5   Where do we discover Holden is, at the end of the novel?

A process of elimination

1   Before Phoebe wakes up, Holden reads her notebooks/writes a note/phones D.B.

2   Phoebe wants Holden to come to D.B.'s movie/her school play/their parents' party.

3   Mr Antolini taught history/English/PE to Holden at Elkton Hills.

4   Holden sleeps on a bench in Central Park/Fifth Avenue/Grand Central Station.

5   Holden shows two boys where to find exhibits of Eskimos/Native Americans/mummies?

Who does this?

1   Who dances to music on the radio?

2   Who wonders if Phoebe has been smoking?

3   Who gives Holden some written advice?

4   Who pats Holden on the head while he sleeps?

5   Who puts the hunting hat on Holden's head in the park?

Holden reaching crisis point

1   What does Holden tell Phoebe he wants to be when he is older?

2   How does Holden react when Phoebe gives him her Christmas money?

3   Why does Holden leave the Antolini's place so suddenly?

4   Why does Holden have trouble crossing the road in Fifth Avenue?

5   When does Holden feel most contented?

Writing essays for exams and coursework

- To prepare for an exam, you should read the text in full *at least twice*, preferably *three* times. You need to know it very well.

- If your text is to be studied for an 'open book' exam, make sure that you take it to the exam. You should not rely too much on the book – you haven't got time. If you are not allowed to take the text in with you, you will need to memorise brief quotations.

- You need to decide fairly swiftly which question to answer. Choose a question which best allows you to demonstrate your understanding and personal ideas.

- Make sure you understand exactly what the question is asking you to do.

- Plan your answer (see page 70.)

- Always have a short introduction, giving an overview of the topic. Refer to your plan as you write to ensure you keep on task. Divide your ideas into paragraphs – without them you may not get above a D. Try to leave time for a brief conclusion.

- Remember: **point–quotation–comment**, e.g. 'Holden is a typical teenager, who uses colloquial language, slang and blasphemy, **[point]** like the word "goddam" **[quotation]**. This was part of his appeal to young audiences in the 1950s, because it was a new approach to literature.' **[comment]**

- The key word in writing essays for exams is timing. You must know how long you have for each question and stick to this.

- Leave yourself a few minutes to check through your work. It does not look impressive if you misspell the names of characters, settings or the author himself.

- Timing is not as crucial for coursework essays, so this is your chance to show what you can really do, without having to write under pressure.

- You can obviously go into far more detail than you are able to in an examination. You should aim for about 1000 words, but your teacher will advise you further.

- If you have a choice of title, make sure you select one that grabs your interest and gives you a lot of opportunity to develop your ideas.

- Plan (see page xx). Make sure that you often refer to the plan and the title as you write, to check that you are not drifting off course.

- Use quotations frequently but carefully and try to introduce them smoothly. It is often effective to quote just one or two words.

- Try to state your own opinion, with phrases such as 'This suggests to me ...'. You will be credited for your ideas, as long as you explain why you think them.

- Putting the novel in context is very important. Include relevant background detail and explain how the cultural and historical setting affects the writer's choice of language.

- Make sure that you include a short conclusion, summing up your key ideas.

- Don't be tempted to copy large chunks of essays available on the Internet. Your teacher will immediately notice what you have done and will not reward it.

- It is a good idea, if possible, to word process your essay. This will enable you to make changes and improvements to your final draft more easily.

Writing essays

1. *You are Phoebe writing your journal after Holden's visit. Explain your concerns about your brother.*

2. *What do we learn about Holden's character from Chapter 1?*

3. *How do Holden's relationships with Jane Gallagher and Sally Hayes help us to understand his character?*

4. *Examine how the city of New York contributes to Holden's growing feelings of depression, confusion and loneliness.*

5. *You are Sally Hayes after your date with Holden. Write a letter to Holden explaining why you think another meeting would be inadvisable.*

6. *Who are Holden's mentors and why do you think they are so important, in their different ways?*

7. *Explore how Salinger depicts different kinds of 'phoniness' in the novel. Remember to refer to specific characters and events in answering this question.*

8. *What, for you, makes* The Catcher in the Rye *such a moving novel?*

9. *How does Salinger make us feel that Holden is unusual as a teenager in America at that time?*

10. *By exploring two characters, show how Salinger reveals different types of student in* The Catcher in the Rye.

11. *How far do you believe Holden is a sympathetic character?*

12. *In A Streetcar Named Desire by Tenessee Williams, one of the characters says; 'I have always relied on the comfort of strangers'. How far does Holden follow this view?*

13. *Holden – hero or victim? Explore the presentation of him in the novel.*

14. *What are the factors that contribute to Holden's breakdown? Do you think it was unavoidable?*

15 You are the head teacher of Pencey Prep. Write a letter to Holden's parents explaining your concerns about his attitude and behaviour.

16 Explore Holden's relationship with his brothers and sister.

17 You are Holden. Write three diary entries covering your experiences in New York after you have left Pencey Prep.

18 How far do you agree that Chapter 26 is a satisfactory conclusion to Holden's journey?

19 Holden has a great empathy with children. Explain how this is shown in the novel.

20 Mr Antolini gives Holden a quotation: 'The mark of the immature man is that he wants to die nobly for a cause, while the mark of a mature man is that he wants to live humbly for one.' How far do you think that this applies to Holden?

21 How does Salinger create such a distinctive voice for Holden through the text of The Catcher in the Rye?

22 Although Holden claims that he is a coward, he seems to provoke violent episodes. Give at least two examples and explain how Holden deals with them.

23 Explore the idea that Holden is on a quest in the novel. What is he searching for?

24 How do you account for the novel's immediate and lasting popularity with young audiences?

Passage-based questions

If, in the exam, you are required to answer a question based on an extract from the novel, make sure you focus on the language used, and also refer to other examples from the rest of the novel. After reading the extract, highlight key phrases to help you write your response.

- It is very important to be organised in your approach. Time spent in planning your response will be reflected in the grade you receive.

- The first thing to do is to read the question very carefully to make sure you fully understand it, and then highlight key words.

- You will need to make some notes on the topic to help you. This can be done in various ways: a list; subheadings; spidergram; or a mind map.

- The advantage of using a mind map or spidergram is that it lets you expand your ideas in a clearly linked, visual way. Put the essay title in the centre of the page. From this a number of key ideas will come out in the form of branches.

- By focusing on each key idea in turn, you will be able to branch out further, as your brain makes connections between the ideas.

- Since mind maps and spidergrams are a way of charting your knowledge, they are also an excellent revision aid. You could work through a number of essay titles in this way. (See some examples of spidergrams on the following pages.)

- Some people prefer to make a mind map even more visual, by colour coding ideas and even adding pictures or symbols.

- In the planning stage of an essay it is also a good idea to jot down some useful quotations. These need not be lengthy and can be added to your mind map.

- Each branch of a mind map might form a separate paragraph in your essay. You can number the branches, so that you are clear about the order of your points. Deal with the main points first.

- Some pupils say that they do not like planning and that they never do so, but he majority of candidates do significantly better when they plan their answers.

Contrasts

- Innocence vs Experience Jane: he was close to her one holiday; knew her well, but not in a physical way; Sally: not as close to her, but they're necking as soon as they get into the cab
- each girl brings out a different side of holden's character
- emphasises his complexity and how mixed up he is

How do Holden's relationships with Jane Gallagher and Sally Hayes help us to understand his character

Sally Hayes 'Queen of the phonies'

- Holden tells us he doesn't like her much
  - BUT he has her picture by his bed at school
  - Is this for show, making him as much of a phony as she is?
- brings out the worst in Holden
  - he uses her for a date because he feels lonely
  - he insults her and abandons her at the ice rink
- associated with the social life of NY: Radio City, Broadway

Jane Gallagher

- associated with Maine; summer holidays; games – tennis, etc.
- Holden sees her as genuine; respects her
- she brings out the best in him
  - he doesn't use her
    - she doesn't appear in person, because Holden shies away from meeting her
    - Is he worried that she'll have changed/ grown up?
  - feels protective towards her
    - suspects stepfather abuses her
    - checkers – she keeps her kings in the back row. A sign of her vulnerability?
      - this emphasises Holden's own vulnerability
      - Holden still thinks about this 18 months later
    - date with Stradlater

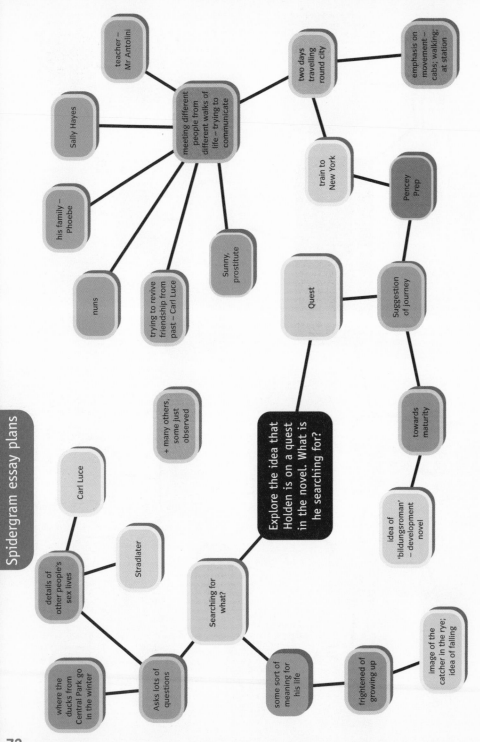

teacher – Mr Antolini

Sally Hayes

his family – Phoebe

nuns

trying to revive friendship from past – Carl Luce

Sunny, prostitute

meeting different people from different walks of life – trying to communicate

two days travelling round city

emphasis on movement – cabs; walking; at station

train to New York

Pencey Prep

Quest

Suggestion of journey

towards maturity

idea of 'bildungsroman' – development novel

+ many others, some just observed

Explore the idea that Holden is on a quest in the novel. What is he searching for?

Carl Luce

Stradlater

details of other people's sex lives

where the ducks from Central Park go in the winter

Asks lots of questions

Searching for what?

some sort of meaning for his life

frightened of growing up

image of the catcher in the rye; idea of falling

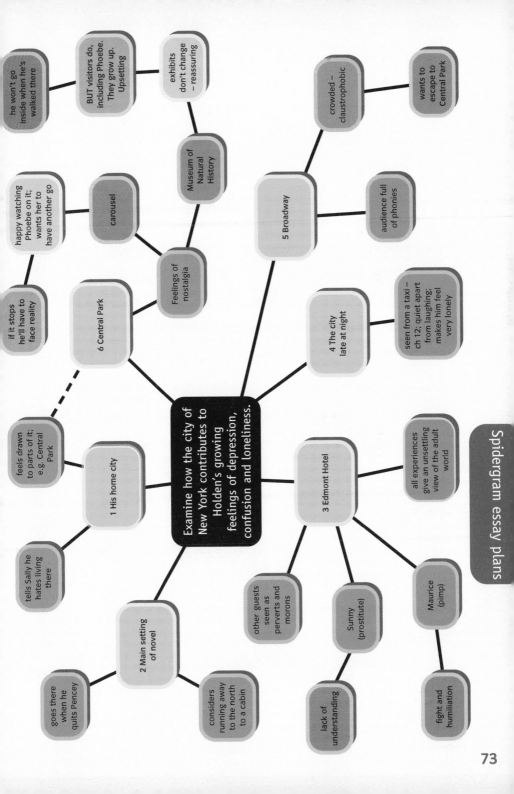

Examine how the city of New York contributes to Holden's growing feelings of depression, confusion and loneliness.

1 His home city
- feels drawn to parts of it; e.g. Central Park
- tells Sally he hates living there

2 Main setting of novel
- goes there when he quits Pencey
- considers running away to the north to a cabin

3 Edmont Hotel
- all experiences give an unsettling view of the adult world
- other guests seen as perverts and morons
- Sunny (prostitute)
  - lack of understanding
- Maurice (pimp)
  - fight and humiliation

4 The city late at night
- seen from a taxi – ch 12; quiet apart from laughing; makes him feel very lonely

5 Broadway
- crowded – claustrophobic
  - wants to escape to Central Park
- audience full of phonies

6 Central Park
- carousel
  - happy watching Phoebe on it; wants her to have another go
  - if it stops he'll have to face reality
- Feelings of nostalgia
- Museum of Natural History
  - he won't go inside when he's walked there
  - BUT visitors do, including Phoebe. They grow up. Upsetting
  - exhibits don't change – reassuring

Sample response

What do we learn about Holden from the opening chapter?

After reading this opening chapter my opinion of Holden changes from dislike at the beginning to sympathy by the end. ✓ At first he seems to be very aggressive and has a low opinion of his parents, even though they are 'nice'. I think that he is trying to gain sympathy from the reader even though he doesn't want us to know too much about his background. ✓ Holden appears to admire his older brother D.B., but he doesn't agree with him moving to Hollywood and 'prostituting' his talents. ✓

He seems to have a bad opinion of his school, Pencey Prep, and the way it advertises itself, although it is probably a very respected school, as most American preparatory schools were. ✓ I think that this is because Holden is a loner and seems to find it difficult to relate to other pupils. ✓ He does, however, form a sort of friendship with Selma Thurmer, the headmaster's daughter, mainly, I think, because he is a teenager and wants a girlfriend, but also because he likes her straight talking.

Holden again gives an example of being an outsider when he misplaces his team's fencing equipment and states that the whole team ostracises him. After telling the reader that he has been kicked out of school he is desperate to think of some happy time to remember the school by and suddenly remembers the time when he was with two other boys playing ball until it got dark. This gives him a good goodbye memory. I think this is because it is one of the few times he can remember being friendly with other pupils. ✓

He goes on to tell the reader about Mr Spencer, his history teacher. I believe that Holden sees him as a sort of father-figure that he needs, not because he hates his own father, but because he can't form friendships very well with people his own age. ✓ In a nutshell, Holden appears to be hinting that he is at a point in his life where his strange personality has driven him to a mental breakdown.

Examiner's comments

This is a solid response, showing clear understanding of the novel and some cultural context. The candidate demonstrates insight into how the character is developed through textual detail and how ideas are conveyed. Points are not developed, however, and need to be supported with quotation. The essay has a clear structure and the candidate remains focused on the title. There is a sense of retelling the story in places, however, and this needs to be avoided. Overall, this is an accurate but under-developed response to the question.

Sample response

What do we learn about Holden from the opening chapter?

Holden is a complex character, ✓ who is the protagonist of the story. The novel opens in a first person narrative style, with Holden engaging the reader in a colloquial, typically American way. He is obviously a teenager, but his constant swearing and blasphemy (quotation) indicates that perhaps he is trying too hard to impress. ✓✓ At first he seems to be very aggressive and has a low opinion of his parents. Likewise, although he appears to admire his older brother D.B., he doesn't agree with him moving to Hollywood and 'prostituting' his talents. Holden seems to think he has the moral upper hand, and it is acceptable for him to criticise those around him, especially close family members. ✓

Holden also has a low opinion of his school, Pencey Prep, and the way it advertises itself, although it is probably a very respected school, as most American preparatory schools were. He loathes the phoniness of it and the way it markets itself. This is one of the on-going themes in the novel and Holden manages to find examples of it everywhere ✓. This may be one of the reasons that Holden is a loner and finds it difficult to relate to other pupils. He does, however, form a sort of friendship with Selma Thurmer, the headmaster's daughter, admiring her straight-talking. ✓

Holden again gives an example of being an outsider when he misplaces his team's fencing equipment and states that the whole team ostracised him. He reveals that the whole incident was funny (quotation), but I think this is bravado, because it would have been very upsetting, especially to someone who is as sensitive as Holden. ✓✓ After telling the reader that he has been expelled from school he is desperate to think of a positive memory of his time at school and poignantly recalls an occasion when he played ball with two other boys until it got dark. (quotation). It is significant that

76

this is the event he chooses, because it is a typical school memory and one where Holden is not being ostracised or ignored. This indicates that he does want and need friends, after all. ✓

He goes on to tell the reader about Mr Spencer, his history teacher. Holden feels obliged to say goodbye to him, which shows he is polite and well brought up. (quotation). Perhaps he has this close relationship with a teacher because he can't form friendships very well with people his own age. ✓

To conclude, the opening chapter serves to introduce Holden directly to the reader. He is presented as if we are in a face-to-face conversation, and, as such, he is being honest. He still, however, tries to impress, but underneath the slang and the cynical attitude there is already a glimmer of the boy who is sensitive and easily troubled. ✓

Examiner's comments

This is well-considered response, which demonstrates an excellent understanding of the main character. The candidate consistently reveals insight into how meaning and ideas are conveyed through language, and refers to textual evidence to support views. Comments are often original and the candidate is not afraid to make connections, or to offer thoughtful ideas. Points are always accompanied by a quotation (which we have been unable to provide here for copyright reasons). The essay is well-structured and there is a neat conclusion firmly based on the title. The candidate remains fully focused.

Answers to quick quizzes

Quick quiz 1
Quick questions
1   Pencey Prep
2   he has failed in most of his subjects; lack of effort
3   a red hunting hat
4   Robert Ackley
5   his brother Allie's baseball mitt

A process of elimination
1   winter
2   the top of a hill
3   fencing
4   the equipment
5   history teacher

Who does this?
1   the fencing team
2   Mr Spencer
3   Stradlater
4   Holden
5   Holden

Establishing Holden's character
1   artificial people – phonies
2   with the peak turned to the back
3   He breaks all the windows in the garage (and tries to break ones in the car).
4   his unclean personal habits
5   his nerves are 'shot'

Quick quiz 2
Quick questions
1   Mrs Morrow, the mother of a classmate
2   checkers
3   Maurice, the lift boy
4   16

A process of elimination
1   Penn
2   the Lavender Room
3   the hotel lobby
4   Maine
5   called him a moron

Take a moment to consider
1   He likes her and does not want to hurt her.
2   He wants to phone someone.
3   His sister, Phoebe.
4   He acts on impulse; he's very depressed.
5   He is dressed in pyjamas.

Who does this?
1   Mrs Morrow
2   the taxi driver
3   Faith Cavendish, the stripper
4   three young women from Washington (in the Lavender Room)
5   Sunny, the prostitute

Impressions of Holden
1   He cannot stop himself once he starts.
2   phony
3   He orders alcoholic drinks and smokes heavily.
4   Allie, his dead brother
5   He pretends that he has been shot in the stomach, as he staggers to the bathroom.

Quick quiz 3

Quick questions
1. Romeo and Juliet
2. *Mercutio*
3. *a record,* Little Shirley Beans
4. *in Central Park – skating on the lake*
5. *He tightens her roller skate.*

A process of elimination
1. *Grand Central Station*
2. *suitcases*
3. *marry her*
4. *ice skating*
5. *Whooton School*

Who does this?
1. *the nuns*
2. *a young boy walking along in the road*
3. *a girl in the Park*
4. *Sally Hayes*
5. *Carl Luce*

Holden in New York
1. *his hunting hat*
2. *The boy is singing for its own sake, not because he's been made to; he's natural.*
3. *It is too crowded – full of people shopping and waiting to go to movies.*
4. *He hates living in New York.*
5. *in case he dies of pneumonia before she has a chance to see him*

Quick quiz 4

Quick questions
1. *she keeps the pieces (puts them in a drawer)*
2. *Robert Burns*
3. *Phoebe*
4. *his hunting hat*
5. *in a hospital/sanatorium, receiving psychiatric help*

A process of elimination
1. *reads her notebooks*
2. *her school play*
3. *English*
4. *Grand Central Station*
5. *mummies*

Who does this?
1. *Holden and Phoebe*
2. *her mother (Mrs Caulfield)*
3. *Mr Antolini*
4. *Mr Antolini*
5. *Phoebe*

Holden reaching crisis point
1. *the catcher in the rye*
2. *he cries*
3. *He suspects that Mr Antolini is making sexual advances.*
4. *He imagines he will fall down and down and never reach the other side.*
5. *when he is watching Phoebe on the carousel*

Page 16, JD Salinger, ©Bettmann/Corbis
Page 19, Scene, ©Bettmann/Corbis

First published 2004

Letts Educational
Chiswick Centre
414 Chiswick High Road
London W4 5TF
Tel: 020 8996 3333

Cover and text design by Hardlines Ltd., Charlbury, Oxfordshire.

Typeset by Letterpart Ltd., Reigate, Surrey.

Graphic illustration by Beehive Illustration, Cirencester, Gloucestershire.

Commissioned by Cassandra Birmingham

Editorial project management by Jo Kemp

Printed in Italy.

British Library Cataloguing in Publication Data. A CIP record of this book is available from the British Library.

ISBN 1 84315 326 2

Letts Educational is a division of Granada Learning, part of Granada plc.